ALSO BY
camilla gibb

Mouthing the Words
The Petty Details of So-and-so's Life
Sweetness in the Belly
The Beauty of Humanity Movement

this
is
happy

a memoir

camilla
gibb

DOUBLEDAY CANADA

Doubleday Canada and colophon are registered trademarks of Random House of Canada Limited.

LIBRARY AND ARCHIVES CANADA CATALOGUING IN PUBLICATION

Gibb, Camilla, 1968-, author
    This is happy / Camilla Gibb.

Issued in print and electronic formats.

ISBN 978-0-385-67812-4 (bound). ISBN 978-0-385-67813-1 (epub)

    1. Gibb, Camilla, 1968-. 2. Authors, Canadian (English)—
20th century—Biography. I. Title.

PS8563.I2437Z53 2014   C813'.54   C2013-906256-4
                                                C2013-906257-2

Text and cover design: Kelly Hill
Cover and text image (egg in nest): Jill Battaglia/Shutterstock.com
Cover background textures: Flas100 and Nik Merkulov, Shutterstock.com
Printed and bound in the USA

Published in Canada by Doubleday Canada,
a division of Random House of Canada Limited,
a Penguin Random House company.

www.penguinrandomhouse.ca

10 9 8 7 6 5 4 3 2 1

this
is
happy

To be rooted is perhaps the most important and least recognized need of the human soul.

Simone Weil

prologue

It is a crisp fall Saturday and I am alone with my daughter, without plans, daunted about getting through the day. My parents have two new cats—I welcome the spontaneous invitation to come over and meet them. My daughter has become a cat herself; it takes two hours to wrangle her into a diaper and a dress, and then the fight over sitting in her car seat begins.

She is two years old. *No, I don't want to, I don't have to, I won't*—she has various ways of expressing a consistent opinion.

It is 11:15 a.m. and we have been up for six hours. We have had a bath and cooked breakfast and made tea and read books and done art and sung songs and played soccer and I am ready for adult company and the distraction of cats and grandparents. But my daughter wants to drive the car. She wants to play with the lock and tune the radio. She wants to do anything but get into her car seat.

I'm promising cats! Grandparents! Riverdale Farm! Goldfish! Dora Band-Aids!

My daughter sits in the driver's seat punching the buttons on the CD player. She helpfully pronounces it broken.

I give up. I sit down on the pavement and tell her I'll wait until she's ready to get into her car seat. I wait a very long time.

Okay, I finally say, standing up, impatient. Would you like to have *my* Saturday? Go for a walk, maybe buy some flowers, a paper and some bread and sit and read for a bit in a café over a coffee?

Yes, she says, much to my astonishment.

So now we are sitting outdoors as I have an Americano and she has a glass of warm milk and a slice of baguette and some fancy French cheese. The basket of my daughter's tricycle holds the pink and yellow flowers she chose from a bucket at the corner store down the street. She eyes me reading my newspaper. Would you like the magazine? I ask.

Yes, she says.

I give her the magazine. She flicks through it, slowing at cleavage and jewels, while I read the paper. Birds hover at her feet, hoping for a crumb. I tell her we can feed the birds, ask her if she wants to. Little pieces, I tell her, they have tiny mouths. She studies them as they snatch the pieces from the ground.

I drink my coffee, scan the newspaper and watch my little girl. You are my daughter, I realize. You are the daughter of someone relatively quiet and tending toward the serious. I'm sorry for not understanding that these things are part of who you are, too. I am sorry for having been so afraid. For having failed to relax enough to know this about you; for having failed to share with you who I am.

We come to know ourselves only through stories. We listen to the stories of others, we inherit the stories of those who came before, and we make sense of our own experiences by constructing a narrative that holds them, and holds us, together. Stories are how we make sense of our lives.

"All sorrows can be borne if you put them into a story or tell a story about them," Isak Dinesen once said. Sorrows are *all* pain otherwise, pain without sense or meaning. But joys, too, it seems to me, need their context. And sometimes their coexistence needs to be borne. The coexistence or possibility of the opposite can be what gives an experience its meaning. At its simplest, that is a story.

And this is mine. It can only be mine, the way I have found to make sense of things. It risks the involvement of others because we do not become ourselves in isolation. Telling such a story, furthermore, relies on memory, that most fallible of sources. It demands the creation of something coherent out of disparate bits and pieces and gaps in knowledge. It is flawed in the way every memoir is inherently flawed. Still, we continue to relate such stories. Because they are necessary. We are the storytelling animal; our stories are what make us human.

part one

incubate

I

I never expected to be happy, to have a sense of belonging somewhere. I didn't grow up with a sense that this was possible or even desirable. I'm quite sure my parents didn't either, so I come by this honestly. Still, they did try to find a way out of what was unhappy. Forty-something years ago, they hatched a plan to escape their English lives. They felt stifled in England, trapped by the expectations of family, of class. They drew up an alphabetical list of Commonwealth countries, ruling out Australia because of distance (and a slight penal twinge), and chose Canada as the place to immigrate with my brother and me, two children under four.

We were too young to understand what was happening. My father came over a year in advance to find a job and a place for us to live. I cried when this strange man lifted me up at the airport. Three months after our arrival, a package arrived from my paternal grandmother. She was a great maker of fudge and had sent us a box of it. I remember the sense of anticipation as my mother peeled back the lid and the collective disappointment as the contents were revealed: green and furry, having spent six weeks on a ship. I understood, somehow, that something between here and there had been broken.

We had no history here, no story of belonging. This disorientation didn't suit my father—a rule-bound, rigid, public-school-educated former British Army officer who had been thrown out of the military for his insult of a black superior. Despite his desire to emigrate to a freer world, his beliefs about race, class, women and children just became more entrenched in Canada. And more obviously peculiar.

I knew he was odd, I knew to tread carefully to avoid being the target of his not infrequent outbursts, but I loved him very much. He scrambled eggs for me, took me swimming and biking, and he played the violin and the guitar. He did puzzles with me and made me look things up in the dictionary. He called me a boisterous girl, a hoyden. He built things out of wood. I liked the smell of sawdust on him and the feel of his cheeks clean-shaven. I loved him even when I was embarrassed by or scared of him. I think I was the only one.

Shortly after our arrival in Canada he was "diagnosed" as being an egomaniac without empathy or regard for others—this by a psychologist hired by his employer to do an assessment of him for some undisclosed reason. My mother tells me my father was enormously proud of this characterization, so much so that he sent a copy of the report home to his parents, this report that pretty much ended his formal working life. After that it was a series of failed attempts to start a business. That and a lot of drinking, and not always getting out of bed.

My mother must have decided she'd had enough. When I was nine, my father went away on a long "business trip." We went to visit him in Chicago over March Break and he asked my mother if she liked the dining-room table and chairs he'd just bought. That furniture told me everything I needed to know. I didn't need to stand outside the next day, staring at a half-frozen pond, having my father spell it out for me.

I didn't want him to be apart from us; I was worried he would be lonely; I was worried I would be lonely, too.

We went back to the apartment, where my brother was so thrilled by the news of their imminent divorce that he was jumping up and down on the bed. My father tended to reserve his cruellest outbursts for my brother. He often referred to him as "that boy," as if to distance himself from their association. He'd take out my mother at the same time. "What's wrong with that boy?" meant *he doesn't get that from my side.* They were a pair, in my father's eyes. And so were we. But from here on the balance would shift.

That same year, a new man, the antithesis of my thin, clean-shaven father, appeared in our lives. Again, I knew what was going on before I was told because of a piece of furniture. My mother took us to an apartment downtown where she was picking up a wooden chest she said she was buying from a friend of a friend.

The apartment smelled of incense and cigarettes. The man was dark, swarthy and very, very hairy. He had scars on his face and spoke loudly with an accent. He was wearing hip-hugging, flared Levi's and a loose white shirt without a collar.

My brother bounced around the place. I crossed my arms over my chest, stood firmly rooted by the door and didn't utter a word.

Ara moved into our house not long after. He was twenty-eight years old, my mother forty. As soon as he arrived, he tossed out the single beds my parents had always slept in and built a double bed. He planted tomatoes and marijuana in the backyard. He was an actor, which wasn't a *real* job, because he didn't wear a suit and go to an office, not that my father had gone to an office in a very long time. Worst of all, he was openly affectionate with my mother.

Everything felt slippery and loose. I didn't like the

changes in the house or the changes I saw in my mother. I missed my father. I felt sorry for him, drunk and crying, living alone, moving constantly—Des Plaines, Long Island, Toronto—or camping in buggy woods or farmers' fields. At school the following year, a teacher I adored pulled me aside and asked me if there was anything wrong at home. I didn't know how to respond. I thought the only legitimate answer, the only right wrong, was that you were being physically abused, which I wasn't. I spent the rest of the year wishing someone would beat the shit out of me so that I could say yes to this teacher. I considered taking a knife and slashing my leg so that I had something to show her, even if I couldn't speak.

At ten years old I was silent and trapped in my own dark fantasies. I watched what was happening around me from a remove.

I saw my brother, who had always been terrified of our father, embrace this new man without hesitation. In fact, everyone did, everyone but me. I kept vigilant, bitter watch for over a year. Then, one weekend, when we were visiting the farm of a friend of my mother's, that changed. I had spent the day swimming solitary laps across the pond while Ara, my brother and a host of other children ran around naked and rolled down the muddy bank. That night there was a wrestling match, and Ara was taken on by the combined forces of four children. From my vantage point on the stairs, as the other children shrieked with delight and pinned him down, I found myself overwhelmed by a surge of proprietary feeling.

It plays out filmically in my memory, in slow and continuous motion. When he was seated again, I stood up. Everyone was silent as I walked across the room toward him. I slid onto his lap. I glared at the other children. He was mine. He belonged to me. The rest of them could just back off.

And suddenly the world brightened; it was brighter than it had ever been. Ara cooked and yelled and danced in our kitchen. He brought noise and colour into our world, as if firecrackers were being let off inside the house. He invited his acting friends over for long dinners and the kitchen was full of food and laughter and wine and smoke. I don't remember my parents ever having anyone over for dinner. There were moments of a kind of happiness, a freedom, that I had never experienced before, the four of us together in bed on Saturday mornings, my mother and Ara reading the paper, my brother and I the comics; there was silliness, and play.

My mother wore a ring Ara had given her and Ara said he wanted to adopt us.

My father referred to Ara as "that Paki your mother was having an affair with while we were still married." The fact that it began as an affair was likely true, but that wasn't what bothered me.

"He's Armenian," I defended. "The Armenians have had a really hard time."

Ara had grown up in Beirut, and he cultivated in us a taste for kibbeh and baba ghanouj and we accumulated a vast arsenal of Arabic words for naughty bodily bits and what one could do with them. Many of these dishes and profanities are still part of my diet and vernacular, even though the man himself is long gone.

He left after just two years of living with us. He squatted on my bedroom floor one night and said things that were probably profound. Crying, he handed me a cheap Avon ring obviously designed for someone with grown-up hands. He was gone the next day. His Ravi Shankar and Arlo Guthrie albums remained in a box in the basement. There was no explanation.

Things at home became sad and quiet. My mother took a frozen lump of something out of the freezer every morning, dropped it in the sink, put on her nylons and her heels and left for work, never returning until the end of the day. She was never sick, never missed a day of work; in duty, perhaps there lay salvation. In the evenings, she cooked the lump, drank two Scotch and sodas and read a book with the cat on her lap.

She has never been much of a talker. She is quiet and concealed, even from her children. At an earlier age, my brother and I found the romance in it. She had worked for MI5 in England. She was a steel trap, which is why she'd made such a good spy. She was the perfect operative:

9

both circumspect and extraordinarily beautiful. She would tell us nothing about her work with MI5. Nothing. This only fuelled our fantasies. She declared she'd only been a secretary. This being classic spy subterfuge, we refused to believe her.

As a consequence of her lack of revelation, I learned to detect the slightest shadow of mood, the obliquest evidence. I felt the hidden things; I absorbed them. Perhaps my mother wanted to spare us her pain by trying to blanket it in silence, but it radiated from her and flooded me.

In order to know someone who is at some level unknowable, you must leave yourself wide open. If you don't, you foreclose the possibility of learning something critical about this person you need, your parent, the person upon whom your survival depends. It's like time-lapse photography; your lens at maximum aperture in order to capture something fleeting and elusive. The problem becomes one of calibration. How to protect yourself in the process. How to capture something without going blind.

My brother and I were ready to receive in a climate of relative deprivation. We were often on our own, latchkey kids, not uncommon in that era. We had inherited my mother's looks: we were pretty children, pretty and vulnerable, my brother particularly so. Once, a stranger stopped him along his paper route and asked if he could show him to a park. My brother said sure, and when they got there the man pulled out his penis and only then did my brother understand something was wrong. My brother fled. My mother called the police. The man was charged with raping two boys in the schoolyard not long after. My brother had to identify him in a lineup.

Right and wrong were clear because he was a boy. For me, things felt much more ambiguous. A man used to stare at me at the swimming pool. He terrified me. He would follow me part of the way home. A man on a schoolyard tennis court called me over to collect a tennis ball, but he was holding his penis in his hand. A teacher wanted to see my belly button, and a later one backed me into a wall and put his tongue in my mouth.

I was frightened, but ashamed in every case, and so I told no one. I both assumed this happened to every girl and assumed it was my fault. The messages we got from my father were very confusing. When, at eleven, I first wore eyeliner, my father called me a slut. When Micah tried to greet my father with a hug, he called him a faggot.

I'd never even kissed a boy. Neither had, or ever would, my brother.

When I was fourteen my mother told me that men were now looking at me rather than her. She implied there was power in this—I have no doubt there had been for her—but all I sensed was danger. I wasn't like her. I wanted it off me. It felt threatening, and I had no idea how I was supposed to respond.

A year later, I was scouted by a modelling agency. I was in no way equipped to handle this kind of career. It ended quickly, the day a photographer ground the hard lump in his pants into my leg.

My brother's first career had come to a similarly abrupt end. He was escorted home one afternoon by two police officers after lifting a cassette tape from a store. He was too young to be charged, so they issued him with a warning.

Between them, my parents must have decided my brother needed a father, or my mother must have decided she could no longer cope—perhaps a bit of both— because Micah suddenly left to live with our father, who had by this point settled on a rundown farm in eastern Ontario. We'd been visiting him there for the past couple of years.

I went to stay with them every other weekend. I wrote poetry by flashlight during the long hours on the Greyhound bus on Friday nights. I'd been writing ever since I learned how to string letters together into words. Stories about icicles with human souls and girls who lived among animals. Poems that got darker and angrier over the years.

My father would pick me up at the Brockville terminal and we would drive another fifty minutes into the black country, where he was drinking a forty-ouncer of gin every day. I never knew which way he was going to swing, what was going to provoke him. He would get hugely enthusiastic about grand schemes that neither money could nor logic would support. I learned not to say the obvious. He built some things, but he destroyed a great many more.

It had always been thus. I remember mornings when he would draw up plans and make lists before the ritual visit to Canadian Tire—all this, a prelude to the massive destruction that would take place in the afternoons. He had torn down a wall in an apartment he had rented in Toronto. Then he'd torn down the ceiling as well, and in its place he'd painted and erected a mural on particle board. It was beautiful—two blue and gold peacocks. It was beautiful—it just didn't make sense.

On the farm, he ripped into a hillside with a backhoe for no apparent reason, felled (illegally) a good number of trees in a government pine plantation and tore down three of the farmhouse's exterior walls. He lived behind tarpaulin, without plumbing or heat. It was dirty and cold and so were we.

He became more bitter and more paranoid with each season. He told me that he was not responsible for anything he said after midday. He mutated throughout the afternoon into something mean and ugly. By night-fall, when his transformation was complete, we were trapped in the one room with heat, a dimly lit kitchen in a haze of wood and cigarette smoke. The world outside the window was silent and black: not even a light from a neighbouring farm in the distance.

My father seethed, skewering us with profanities. The thrust of his diatribes was that he had found us out, he was on to us, our "game." He could see straight into our perverse minds, he knew just what we were thinking, he could see how we were manipulating people for our own deviant purposes, how we thought we had him fooled. It was the extreme version of a theory he seemed to have been developing over the years.

We cried silently into our laps, and the more upset we became, the crueller he would get. We made ourselves small, becoming shrivelled remnants of ourselves.

My brother stayed at the farm for two years, breaking the ice on top of the well on winter mornings, taking a shower at the Texaco station once every two weeks, being bullied at school, worse at home.

Every time I arrived at the farm, I asked my father to hide his bullets, keeping them well away from his hunting rifle. I was a sleepwalker. And he'd taught me how to shoot.

You may wonder where my mother was in all this. I actually wonder, too. Did she pick me up from the bus station on Sunday nights? I suppose so, though I have no recollection of it. What did I tell her about these weekends?

I was an angry teenager. A teenager built on the sullen and withdrawn back of a child. I can't have been easy to love. I suspect I told her nothing.

What did my brother tell her on his visits home? I assume very little. He would begin to speak of his time in the country only years later, and even then, he would swear me to silence, prefacing anything he was about to divulge by threatening to kill me if I told our mother.

He wanted to protect her. We both did. We wanted to protect her not just from unhappy stories but from the destructive potential in ourselves. She gave us physical safety, worked hard to keep us housed, fed and clothed, saved money to send us to camp and to visit relatives in England, all without any financial help from my father. We couldn't burden her with more, with evidence of the increasing cruelty and eccentricity of the man she'd freed herself from. With evidence of disturbance in our own souls. We couldn't afford to lose her.

Years later, my brother would say of his time at the farm: There was nowhere for me to run. There were only trees. Miles and miles of nothing. I used to stare at the trees and realize I was trapped. There was just nowhere to run.

I think a piece of my brother died out there.

I had my notebook, but Micah had no refuge. Until at fifteen, he found his in drugs.

2

Growing up, I was quite sure I would never have children. I didn't have fantasies of marriage and motherhood. Perhaps the rupture of my own family destroyed my confidence in the idea of one. Perhaps I was just too dark to embrace the necessary light. There has long been a strain of nihilism in me that wonders what we all amount to in the end and why, indeed, we bother.

During the course of my graduate work in England in my mid- to late twenties, I found myself in the midst of a long and major depression. I did not *fall* into it, there was no tumble, just this sense of numbness and dread within and all around me as if it had always been there. I didn't know then that this was depression. I just knew it was best that I keep my head down and do my work. As a master's student this meant presenting a paper to my tutor each week. After that weekly meeting, my friend Sarah and I would go to the pub together and lose our minds for a night before starting research for the following week's paper the next day. This meant trudging to the Bodleian Library in the inevitable and unremitting drizzle, ordering books that would take two days for a librarian to unearth from the catacombs and returning to my room in residence in the interim to think through questions like: what is a person?

I wrote a reasonable essay in response to that question while feeling I was becoming less and less of a person myself.

I had come to England possessed with some fantasy that I was of this place; that I would feel, at some deep level, a sense of origin and continuity, some affinity that could root me; some attachment. I had often wondered how different a person I would be if I had grown up here instead of in Canada.

But Oxford was the worst place to bring any fantasy of belonging. It is a cold and competitive environment that demands not just intellectual rigour but a resilience best served by the privilege and entitlement only a certain pedigree can engender.

I tried to put these realities to one side as I went about the business of pursuing a very good education. But I soon began to feel I was really nothing more than a brain in a box. I questioned whether I even had a body anymore. When I walked down the street, I felt not just unseen but unseeable. I had a sense that I was breaking up into pixels, no longer a coherent whole.

Perhaps it was the need to know whether I still had a body that led me to open my door to relative strangers: my door, my bed, my legs. To men, women, couples. The net result of a lot of random sex was that what was left of me disappeared.

I became convinced that I must have inherited my father's illness, whatever that might be. At ten, I had diagnosed him as an alcoholic, but even then I knew it wasn't simply the bottle. At Oxford, I started to read in search of answers. I spent hours squatting on the floor of the psychiatry section at Blackwell's bookshop looking up symptoms and signs. I read about schizophrenia and manic depression and various disorders of the self, and although I knew my father had had a penchant for killing small animals as a child—a classic sign of psychopathology—I was too scared to pursue that line of inquiry any further.

My father never sought any help. He was immensely suspicious of any kind of authority. Once, he and my brother had both become ill on the farm after eating some chicken my father had wrapped in tinfoil and chucked into a fire—his preferred method of cooking. (I can still feel that particular combination of charred skin and blood in my mouth; in fact, I am nostalgic for it in the way I am for anything he cooked: burnt toast with Marmite, boiled ground beef.) I was not with them on this occasion. I took my brother to a clinic when he was back home for a weekend, and he was diagnosed with salmonella. My father refused to see a doctor. If he would never let a doctor near his body, he certainly wouldn't let one into his mind.

My master's program was coming to an end while I was unravelling. Those weekly papers were read and discussed but never graded. The entirety of the degree rested on two days of exams and a take-home essay at the end of the year. After the second day of exams, I took a walk to Port Meadow—flat, often flooded and shrouded in mist. Lewis Carroll began *Alice's Adventures in Wonderland* here, rowing up the Isis with the Liddell sisters. I stood on Walton Well Road Bridge. There was a Roma caravan at the end of the bridge, horses in the meadow to my right, but I was staring at the canal and the train tracks running below.

You'd do little more than break your legs by jumping off it, I thought.

I'd never had a thought like that before. Unfortunately, once you admit possibilities like these into consciousness, they never leave. They are always there, dangling at the outer reaches; they can even become a source of comfort.

I had some friends who lived near the meadow, in a depressing nineteenth-century industrial block of unheated houses owned by an ironworks factory. I left the bridge with my new thoughts and walked to their house. One of them was a social worker and I told her how I was feeling. She suggested I speak to a psychiatrist, and we made an appointment at the Warneford, a psychiatric hospital, for the next day.

From the outside, the hospital looked just like you'd imagine a former lunatic asylum should. I have a memory of stepping inside, the height of the atrium, the quality of its light, but no memory of the particular psychiatrist I saw. I didn't know then that I was crossing a threshold into a world of mental illness. There would be several more psychiatrists over the years; they rather began to bleed together.

I remember answering questions about myself and my family, a doctor creating a psychiatric profile. I was asked whether I had ever heard voices. Whether I had ever believed I was governed by forces outside myself.

These are complicated questions. You know that answering yes marks you as a particular kind of crazy. You know that answering no doesn't tell the whole story. But there is no answer halfway between—at least not in psychiatry. Once, was my answer. Once, about three years before, I had felt I was being drawn somewhere not of my own volition.

———

I had fallen in love in my second-last year of high school. David was two years older, a math and physics major at the University of Toronto. We met through music. He was an exceptional flautist and understood music in the innate way he understood math. I was an unexceptional violist, drifting away from school.

David took me by the shoulders and asked me what I was planning on doing with my life. He was the only person who had ever asked. He was concerned: he said I was smart but seemed completely lost. I had dropped out of more than half my classes. I had no answer for him.

David's parents were both social scientists. I wasn't sure what this meant, except that at the dinner table they discussed interesting, worldly things: AIDS in Africa, female circumcision, politics, the environment. They had lived in Paris. They drank wine with dinner. It was so unlike the world in which I'd grown up that I sat in mute, intimidated silence.

The summer after we met, David got a job in Nairobi working for a Swedish development organization. I joined him in July.

We took an overnight train to the Swahili coast, David and I in separate cars for men and women. I shared chapattis and rice, tea and sandwiches with the three Indian women in my sleeping cabin. David and I stayed in a small and basic hotel on the dhow-spotted Indian Ocean. I had never been anywhere so other and so beautiful in my life. We read *Robinson Crusoe* aloud to each other on the beach and made a promise that wherever life took us we would meet here, in this exact spot, in twenty years.

For David's twentieth birthday, we took a Jeep from Nairobi down into the Rift Valley, descending six thousand feet from the cloud-covered capital into an arid plane dotted with extinct volcanoes. I stood in the midst of a salt flat in the punishing sun, wondering how people survived here. The NGO David was working for was concerned with how deforestation was turning arable land into desert. It was a shock to me, the idea of the encroaching desert, a problem largely of our own making. I knew then, right there in that salt flat in the Rift Valley, that I was going to become a social scientist like David's parents.

By the end of that summer David and I had planned our lives together. I had a year of high school left in which to redeem myself. I would move into David's parents' house and change schools. For the first time in my life I had a sense of agency, of direction, albeit very much tied to David and his parents. My mother seemed to see the wisdom in this move.

Shortly after I moved into David's parents' house, my father turned up in Toronto. He had left the farm in eastern Ontario—simply stepped away from it, unable to afford to keep it any longer, left all the family heirlooms he'd taken from his parents, just abandoned it all. He was squatting in a warehouse on Cherry Beach. He came over one summer night when David's parents were away.

He drank a bottle of their gin. He told me I would be "scrounging off the state" by going to university; *he* was a man of too much pride for such a thing. He was going to start a business installing security systems for sliding glass doors. He'd invented the product. He was going to make money. *That's* what it was all about. He wandered off down the alleyway at the side of the house that night, neglecting to say goodbye.

He called me the next day to ask if I could ask David's parents whether he could live in their house, too.

I didn't know what to do. He was my father. He had nowhere to live. David was not confused. "It's completely inappropriate of him to ask," he said.

The next day I stammered: "It's not my place, Dad. I'm a guest here."

"Right," he said.

"But Dad?" I pleaded.

"Nuff said." And then he hung up the phone.

I would later hear from my brother that my father had "disowned" me.

In our Kenyan-inspired master plan, David and I had decided to do our graduate work in England, both of us having been born there. But over the next couple of years, as his interests became more specialized, it became apparent he would be better off in the States. So in the late summer of 1989, we packed up his Honda Civic and drove from Toronto to L.A., arriving at his graduate residence with just two days left until my flight back to Toronto. We weren't talking about the imminent fact of our separation, but in less than a week we would be halfway round the world from each other. I was going to Cairo. We had been inseparable for four years. Now we wouldn't see each other for nine months.

I was doing my undergraduate degree in social anthropology and Middle Eastern studies—an interest that had been ignited by Ara. I had retained such strong memories of Ara's passion and the contrast of his culture with mine, and I wanted to immerse myself in a richer world, study Arabic, learn about Islam, explore the Sahara Desert.

David and I watched movies for those two days in his tiny room in residence. It felt terribly melancholic, sitting in the blue light while the Californian sun blazed outside. He drove me to the airport. I cried, suddenly remembering that I'd left the ring he'd given me, the one I always wore, on the edge of the sink in his bathroom.

"Tell me it's not an omen," I said.

"It's not an omen," he assured me.

I spent the first month in Cairo in tears. I was overwhelmed by this seething, heaving mass of a city and I didn't think I could navigate my way through all its strangeness without David. He was my compass: he had been for years—my compass, my partner, my family, my friend.

I did begin to find my way—I loved the desert, but I can't say I ever acclimatized to the city. David would be joining me in June; that was what kept me looking forward. Then, in May, he suddenly said he wouldn't be able to come. In June, he gave up his apartment and left no forwarding address, no phone number. I began to spin. I couldn't face the thought of my life without David.

After the term ended, instead of going home I went to the Sinai Peninsula with two American friends from the university. In Dahab, I met a soft, barefoot guitar-playing Israeli who rescued me from a very intense and beefed-up Egyptian man I'd made the mistake of kissing. We spent a reckless summer together, camping among lost souls on beaches on either side of the border. We weren't in love, we weren't happy. I was simply avoiding my life. I'm not sure what Lev was up to.

But I did eventually have to leave—my last year of classes was starting soon. I booked my ticket home. Lev said he would earn enough money to come to Canada. I was relieved when I got on that bus back to Cairo alone. But then I got hauled off that bus at gunpoint in the middle of the Sinai Desert. Visiting Israel had invalidated my Egyptian student visa. I would miss my flight home. I had to return to Israel, and to the Israeli.

I didn't feel I was in control of any of this. I thought, for a time, that Lev was. It was his power—a force of good or evil, I didn't know which—that was forcing me back. I actually believed there was something supernatural at work. I felt that my only way out of the Middle East would be with him.

Lev asked me to marry him. I said yes. We celebrated our engagement in Dahab by passing out sweets to the Bedouin children peddling clothes along the beach. Then he took me home to Dimona, one of the settlement towns built in the 1950s to house the influx of North African Jews who fled to Israel after the war of 1948. It was a hostile and poor city of barred and graffiti-covered housing blocks in the middle of the Negev Desert. It was the most depressing place I had ever seen.

Lev's mother was tiny and wrinkled and kind, and as soon as he introduced me as his fiancée, she led me straight to the linen closet. She proudly pointed out gifts for the marital home. I suppressed a feeling of panic. I wanted to run, but I was afraid of this place, of the town beyond the barred windows of his mother's apartment.

That night, I asked Lev if we could leave. In the morning we left for Tel Aviv so that we could both apply for Egyptian visas. During the two-week wait for our passports, we camped on an Israeli beach with drifters and addicts and tattooed ex-cons, living on crackers and baked beans. I hated it. And I started to hate him.

With our passports back, we took a taxi through the desert into the Sinai. "I want to give you a baby," he whispered into my ear as we huddled in the back seat.

I stared at the back of the head of the Bedouin driver for a moment and then said: "Are you crazy?"

He laughed and said yes, that's why he didn't have to do military service.

I bought a ticket home. Lev sold his guitar and his jeans and had enough money for a ticket to England, where I would be changing planes.

At Heathrow he said he was going to head up north to work with an old friend and earn the money to get to Canada. I wasn't sure whether the friend up north existed, but I left him at the airport. I received a postcard a year later. "I am Lev. I am in Greece. I miss you." I never heard from him again.

Ever since, I have had a recurring dream that I cannot escape the Middle East. That I have seven passports in my purse and none of them are mine.

Once, was the short answer I gave to the psychiatrist who asked if I had ever felt I was being controlled by outside forces.

On the basis of this and what I relayed about my father's history, I was diagnosed as having a bipolar disorder. I was now officially mentally ill. I would take lithium and an antidepressant and see a psychiatrist and have my lithium levels measured once a month.

I went back to Canada for the rest of the summer, telling no one at home about my diagnosis. I listened to my brother's unhappy stories instead. He had left his girlfriend and was sleeping in the park. Worst of all, he was getting into fights, fights he knew he could not win— provoking bigger men into beating the shit out of him. He did not understand why; he knew only that he needed to be beaten up.

In our early twenties, we were both losing our minds. My brother's situation broke my heart. He had been such a beautiful boy, such an innocent, so wide open. Put that defenceless spirit in the hands of an abusive man and it will not survive. Soul murder is a term I have heard used.

3

In September I went back to England to start my PhD. Where my master's degree had entailed a weekly meeting with my tutor, the PhD program involved contact only when I sought it. I had no trouble being self-motivated and working for long stretches on my own, but it brought with it an unhealthy isolation.

I was doing research about a walled Muslim city in Ethiopia—a fabled and mysterious place. I read every historical source about this city and chased down the little that had been written about it in the current era. I found a dictionary that had been compiled by a linguist in the 1950s and attempted to extract from this some understanding of the grammar of the unwritten Harari language. I wrote to priests and historians and Hararis in Ethiopia and abroad.

The research was fascinating, but whenever I took a break from it I found myself thinking about suicide. It seemed possible, I don't know how, to hold these contradictory possibilities of the future in my head.

There were no bridges high enough in Oxford, but there was a fast train to London. Yet what if I made a miscalculation and ended up a quadriplegic for the rest of my life? Then I wouldn't even have the mobility to try again.

I don't remember the precipitating moments, but one night, only weeks after returning from Canada, I sat on the carpet in my flat on the top floor of an old man's house and took all my lithium tablets, antidepressants and sleeping pills. I sat there calmly waiting to feel something. And then I worried I hadn't taken enough and swallowed a bottle of Tylenol. And then I still worried I hadn't taken enough and would end up brain damaged for the rest of my life, which seemed a worse outcome than being a quadriplegic, but I had nothing left to take.

I called my friend Sarah. She rang for an ambulance. She came to my flat. I wouldn't know this for another day because I missed these events entirely.

I have a memory, hazy and yet distinct, of a tube being down my throat and a doctor counting pills as they rattled up the plastic, becoming more and more lucid, a kind nurse holding my hand and saying my name. I spent what remained of the night on a bed in an area beside a nurses' station. Four other people were there in beds, too, one of them a woman who had broken both her legs after jumping off a bridge not high enough. I heard another woman howling like a wounded animal. Then I saw a nurse at the end of my bed. She was repeating my name. That awful sound was coming from me.

I was admitted to the psychiatric hospital in the morning. I had no fear of the place, no expectations about it—nothing, really, beyond a kind of numb disbelief that this was another day, that the world just went on like this, day after day, regardless of how you felt or where you had spent the night.

I had a room to myself in the women's ward: sterile, comfortable, a window in the door so a nurse could look in every fifteen minutes until I graduated from suicide watch to something else. There was a cafeteria for meals, a kitchen where you could make yourself a cup of tea or Ovaltine or toast, spreading your butter and Marmite with a plastic knife. The bathroom had a long piece of tin rather than a mirror, which gave you back only the vaguest reflection of yourself. There was a TV room where we all smoked.

The ward housed women of all ages, in all states of dress, but I only really noticed the ones who looked to be about my age. The obese Sri Lankan woman who didn't talk but played the piano. The slow-motion, broken bird of a girl named Jo who was afraid to wash her hair and needed to be held all the time, and frequently sat down in my lap, which I didn't mind. The anxious and animated American woman named Morgan who would suddenly lapse into a daze in the middle of a conversation.

After dinner we all lined up for our medication— Smartie time, Jo called it. One night I stared, horrified, fascinated, at a woman lying on the floor in the hall repeating things, rhyming words, mostly expletives.

"What's wrong with her?" I asked the nurse, as she checked off my name on a list and handed me a little paper cup.

"Manic," she said.

Oh, I remember thinking, so that's what it looks like. I dutifully swallowed my pills.

The staff psychiatrist had changed my medication, or rather, added to it. Two antidepressants now, in addition to the lithium and sleeping pills. Did it make me feel any better? I have no idea. I felt quite calm in hospital, safe, relieved to be sequestered from my life beyond. My mother didn't know where I was, which allowed me to maintain some fiction that this wasn't quite real. I knew I wasn't nearly as sick as some people, but I didn't feel uncomfortable or out of place.

One day, perhaps a couple of weeks after being there, I said to a nurse that I wanted to go outside for a walk. She granted me outside privileges, and I was allowed to wander the grounds. I came across the woman who had broken both her legs. She hissed at me and said: "I put you in here."

"What are you talking about? You have nothing to do with me being here," I said.

"It was all those times I was calling you a cunt," she said. "Only you couldn't hear me."

It was the only moment during that time in hospital that I felt scared. It was also the only time that I thought: *crazy*.

I had visitors during those weeks: Sarah, my tutor, and a professor from my college. He brought me a bag of plums and told me that when he was an undergraduate they used to consider this place just another Oxford college, given how many students you could find here at any given time. He made me laugh and he let me beat him at pool.

One day Jo, Morgan and I went on a field trip with a nurse. We went to Oxfam and rifled through the second-hand clothes and books. We had lunch together in the world. Later that week I told the nurse stationed at the door that I was going for a walk outside, and she said: "You look nice. You're wearing lipstick."

I felt embarrassed. But I knew then that I was ready to leave this place, and that it showed.

Sarah came to collect me when I was discharged. We went for dinner at a Lebanese restaurant. A man at the next table caught my eye—brooding, handsome and intense, his masculinity offset by a lavender sweatshirt and big blue eyes framed with feather-like lashes. I wrote a note saying I'd like to meet him. I left it with the waiter to give to him after Sarah and I had left.

Ted called me the following week and invited me for a drink. At a bar in North Oxford he told me he didn't usually drink because of the medication he was taking. He said he'd been depressed for seventeen years. I told him about my very recent history. He told me about his recent hurts. And then we both proceeded to drink rather a lot.

Two weeks later, he asked me to move in with him and I did.

Once a month I went to the hospital for a blood test. I answered routine questions asked by a different psychiatrist each time. I was depressed but never manic. Having seen in hospital what that looked like, I wasn't sure I ever had been. But the fact that I could keep on working as I did suggested to the professionals that I was. I often worked intensely to the exclusion of everything else. But this was Oxford. You don't get to Oxford, or survive it, by doing anything less.

My tutor had not been wrong to refer to the Warneford Hospital as an Oxford college. The university wasn't unaware of the pressure put upon students. Each year there were inevitably suicides by high-achieving students, and residence dons were newly required to look out for and report the signs of depression. At my college, Magdalen, if you wanted to climb the clock tower, you had to have a letter declaring your mental rather than your physical fitness.

I began to wonder whether my diagnosis hadn't been a bit overzealous. I had doubts, but it wasn't the time to raise them. I was soon going to be leaving for a year of field research in Ethiopia. It was time to assure psychiatrists that I was quite sane enough for the undertaking. They couldn't stop me from going, but they could refuse to write a prescription for such a large number of pills.

When I left for Ethiopia, I took two black duffle bags with me: one full of clothes and books, the other stuffed with ramen noodles, powdered soups and a year's worth of psychopharmaceuticals.

4

I travelled from Addis Ababa overland to Harar, 518 kilo-metres on broken roads over three days. I was dropped off in Harar's main square, where I stood holding a let-ter of introduction to the family of a museum curator with whom I'd been corresponding. My arrival didn't go unnoticed. Within a few minutes, someone turned up to collect me and take me to Haji Mohammed and Fatuma Sitti's house.

They were a respectable couple in their mid-fifties: he had made the pilgrimage to Mecca, and she was a direct descendant of the Prophet Mohammed. He was a cloth merchant, and she owned a farm outside the city. They had nine children, including two daughters living in the United States, from whom they received regular remittances. Perhaps that is why they were willing to risk the attention they would inevitably draw to themselves by taking in a foreigner. I was a complete aberration in this place; the only foreigner for miles.

I paid rent, observed a curfew, dressed modestly and wore a veil and inhabited the women's quarters along with Fatuma Sitti, her twenty-one-year-old daughter, Ekram, and any visiting female neighbours or relatives. We slept on red-clay platforms and passed a water jug between us in the courtyard in order to bathe. We ate all our meals together, sharing one bowl of watery, fenugreek-laden stew twice a day, fishing for tiny morsels of carrot and potato with our right hands. The women ate, slept and prayed together in one room; Haji Mohammed and their older sons in another room across the courtyard. The world was cleaved in two, with the exception of the younger boys, who moved freely in between.

We lived like any other family, sharing triumphs, tribulations, news and the mundane details of daily life. After dinner the boys came to me for help with their English homework. The women helped me with my Harari. Ekram and I gossiped in broken English: I told her about my boyfriend; she told me about hers. Ted existed for me in a faraway place, a place where I'd been very unhappy. While I missed him at times, I did not miss the person I was with him; I felt more alert and alive than I had in a very long time.

I was still taking a great trough of medication each morning. Even though I'd never felt the drugs had offered me any relief, I was afraid to change that regimen so far away from home. I was also, like most people in the city, chronically ill. It was principally a problem of water—the brown, intermittent supply of it from the pump that we drank and cooked with, washed dishes and bathed in, before throwing it out into the street where it trickled downhill and seeped into the ground. We drank tea and ate stew every day made with that brown water.

There was a fly-filled pit latrine, rats and flying cockroaches. There was leprosy, TB, hepatitis, HIV. We all had bloated, gaseous bellies and severe diarrhea courtesy of intestinal parasites. We routinely killed the parasites by taking expired antibiotics sold singly along-side pieces of chewing gum and individual cigarettes in the makeshift stalls that lined the main street.

I got better at interpreting the early signs of parasitic invasion, but I didn't always catch it in time. When I failed to, I would get dizzy and my vision would begin to blur. I assumed this happened to everyone, except that on the worst of these occasions, I could see I was suffering differently. My hands had begun to tremble just like they did in the early days of taking lithium. The drug can be toxic, and I was pretty sure that the dehydration that results from chronic diarrhea had increased the lithium concentration in my blood. I was showing all the signs of blood poisoning, and that scared me enough to go to the local hospital.

In a crumbling old Italianate building, I paid the hospital fee and sat on a bench against a wall of peeling green paint, waiting hours before seeing a doctor. Dr. Hassan was a tall, dark-skinned twenty-four-year-old who spoke excellent English. His soft voice contradicted his size. He was wearing a grey suit under his white coat, and proper laced-up shoes as opposed to the flip-flops I was wearing and had come to think of as national dress. He was back in his hometown for a year of mandatory community service after his medical training at Addis Ababa University. He had had only one training session in psychiatric illness and no clinical practice in the subject. He had no means of testing my lithium levels, but he listened and empathized as I revealed a deeply incriminating secret: a mental illness in a country where the crazy are hidden from view or, if they are without family, left to roam the streets. I was telling him something about the woman I had left behind in England, the woman under this veil. He was interested and completely unfazed.

I realized that my only option was to simply stop taking lithium. I decided I'd rather take that risk than die of blood poisoning in a remote Ethiopian city.

I was sick for a week and a half as the lithium left my system. I wanted to lie in the dark with a sheet over my head, sleep in silence, daydream, but this was not the

Harari way. To be alone is to invite evil spirits, so the women in the neighbourhood kept me company, sitting around my prostrate body, singing songs together, weaving baskets, burning incense, sorting through grains. A tiny girl from the neighbourhood, a girl they called Biscutti, crawled over me, tickled me, hid under the sheet.

Fatuma insisted I was sick because when I first arrived I didn't wear trousers under my skirts. Someone must have resented my bare skin and cursed me with the evil eye. Aini, her sister, said I was sick because I wasn't Muslim enough. She threw down a prayer rug and pointed in the direction of Mecca. "But I'm not Muslim at all," I protested weakly. "Well, then?" they shouted. "What more proof do you need?"

Dr. Hassan came to see how I was. He lived with his aunt and uncle just down the street, it turned out. Fatuma Sitti was impressed to discover I had such respectable friends. He took some tea from her and we had a talk about his medical training, his ambitions. He dreamt of doing specialized training in the States. He was busy preparing for the exams he was going to take in Cairo in a year's time, the final stage in a special scholarship competition for African doctors. He had made it this far; he thought he stood a chance. He was at a certain disadvantage, though, not having the textbooks he needed to study. I was sure I'd be able to find them in England and promised to send them when I returned home in a few months' time.

Finally I felt better, and much to my relief, my mood hadn't plummeted. Or soared. I was eager to get back to work. I was interested in speaking with local midwives and I had started by interviewing the midwife I knew in our neighbourhood: Biscutti's grandmother.

Biscutti and her parents were desperately poor, supported only by the grandmother's paltry income. Their house had a dirt floor; a patch of ground behind it was where they went to the bathroom. I would often find Biscutti sitting alone in the road eating dirt—a disorder called pica, often a sign of iron deficiency. But it can also be a sign of developmental issues. She was nearly three, but she hadn't started speaking yet, she didn't interact with other children, and open wounds on her face refused to heal.

She'd taken to spending a couple of hours with me nearly every day. I gave her crayons and filled buckets with hot water that I warmed over the fire so I could bathe her. I washed her clothes. She was a wordless holy terror, eating crayons, splashing water and tearing up my notebooks when I wasn't looking. She would leave for home when she realized that no amount of tugging on my breast was going to yield milk.

I'd never had a relationship with a child before. I didn't know many children, and in my rare encounters with them I had always felt awkward and inadequate. But in Ethiopia, I was in general less self-conscious and inhibited. I had no choice but to interact—my survival depended on it. And I felt liberated by the truth that in this place, no matter how much I studied the language or learned and adopted the ways of the culture, I could only ever be an aberration. I had found a place where it was appropriate, sane even, to feel like a foreigner.

I was a source of curiosity and suspicion for many, but among those close to me, more one of novelty and amusement. I made people laugh with my mistakes. My first attempt to describe a stomach ache came out as: the foreigner has a war inside the stomach. People greeted me thereafter: How is the war? And I would answer: There is peace now, Alhamdulillah, and you?

With Biscutti in particular I was free to make a fool of myself: rattling the bars of her wordless prison, try-ing to shake her loose. I often carried her around on my hip when I ran errands—going to the market for vege-tables or qat, a leaf chewed as a stimulant. The qat sellers mocked me: Why do you go around with that filthy child? Why do you choose that one—she is just a poor nothing. I couldn't explain that somehow we had chosen each other.

The sores on Biscutti's face kept getting worse, and I decided to take her to Dr. Hassan. He gave me some antibiotic ointment to apply twice a day, and while I held her, he painted her face with purple anaesthetic. We stood as close as two people can be with a baby between them; too close for an unmarried man and a woman in this Muslim town.

He invited me to a *bercha* on the weekend—a qat party, where people recline on pillows, drink tea, talk and chew this semi-narcotic leaf with some determination until the point when they are silent and high.

The *bercha* at his house was a sultry affair. It was conducted in a hidden room because the company was mixed sex, young men and women, highly charged. It was conducted in the dark because Hassan had something very rare: a television and a VCR. We watched an American thriller, the name of which I forgot because all I was conscious of was Hassan, cross-legged and breathing beside me in the dark.

When the lights came on, we talked about some of the work I was doing with midwives. He offered to accompany me on visits to the Oromo midwives I had not been able to interview because I didn't speak their language, a language he, like most Hararis, spoke.

We started to do interviews together every Saturday after that, and at the house of the last Oromo midwife I interviewed, I found myself holding my breath as Hassan stroked the foreheads of two girls who had just been infibulated. He told the two girls they were brave, and we fed them honey with a spoon.

At his *bercha* the next day he found my hand in the dark. His hand was large and warm. He wrote a note: *I love you.* I wrote back: *I love you too.* We couldn't speak. In fact, we didn't ever speak it. We were in love with things far more complicated than each other.

After all his friends had left we kissed in the dark room strewn with qat branches. And then I left with my pounding heart, pulling my veil over my head, making my way down the road home, trying not to give it all away to my "parents" with my face.

But Ekram, my sister and confidante, knew. She knew that look.

"You know he cannot marry you," she said.

Take me with you, sponsor me, get me a visa, people started to say to me as my time in Harar was nearing its end. I tried not to make promises I wouldn't be able to keep. Some people began to treat me as if I had already left. Biscutti, for instance, stopped coming to visit. Her mother said it was because she knew I was leaving.

"But how can she know?"

"Because you took her photograph," Nunu said. "Don't leave her. Take her to England with you."

When I told Nunu that I couldn't take her daughter from her, she responded with an accusation: "You don't really love her."

"She's being realistic," Hassan later said. "She wants a better life for her child. And you could give her that."

Realistic? The only way I could imagine this happening was if he and I married and adopted Biscutti together. That fantasy took hold of my imagination. When I got to Addis I would ask the Canadian embassy about adopting a baby. Perhaps Hassan and I would find ourselves making a life together in Baltimore or Boston when he got his scholarship to study in the States.

But we never spoke about the future. I didn't really even speak about my parallel present: the life I'd left behind in England, my boyfriend, Ted. When it came time for me to return to England, by way of Addis Ababa, he said that he would take me to the airport in Dire Dawa, about an hour away from Harar. We had to travel separately. Ekram saw me into a taxi and disappeared into the bustle of the market. When the taxi arrived in Dire Dawa, Hassan was waiting in the square.

We spent two nights together outside the walls, then we took a taxi to the airport. Still we said nothing about the future. We said nothing other than goodbye.

5

In that brief journey between the walls of an Ethiopian city and those of an English swamp, I was alone in a way I had not been for a year—an invitation to evil spirits. You cannot adopt a baby who has parents, a staffer at the embassy in Addis had told me. And there was the very likely possibility that I would never see Hassan again. Who could I even tell of Hassan's existence? How would I reconcile these two lives; who in England would ever forgive me? In addition to my boyfriend, there was my supervisor and the rest of my department, all of us bound by the cardinal rule of fieldwork: do not sleep with the natives.

I'd seen my supervisor in Addis a few months before, when she was on her way to southwestern Ethiopia. I had flown to the capital to meet her in the lobby of the Ghion Hotel.

I adored this awkward and deeply intellectual woman. She was a student of the great colonial father of British social anthropology, Edward Evan Evans-Pritchard, and she had taught at the University of Khartoum when she was my age. Now, nearly sixty, she was headed for a remote place called Bonga and she was very proudly telling me about her new tent.

As we were sitting in the hotel lobby, a noisy parade of women in glittering veils approached. Relatives of the family with whom I lived in Harar had come to meet me with baskets and pots of food to take back to their families. I remember the look of amazement on my supervisor's face, and her comment that I really seemed to have ingratiated myself within this community. I thought this was a compliment. But then later that evening, she asked me why I was living with a family, why I didn't have my own space apart, some privacy. I was shocked by the question. How could you learn about people, their culture, their language, if you didn't live among them? In hindsight I wondered if she had perhaps been cautioning me in her very English way: there can be such a thing as too much immersion.

My life in Ethiopia had felt real and happy. The only problem was—it wasn't my life.

I got drunk on the plane, trying to blur the passage, swallow it all down, gripped by fear of the crushing, familiar grey that is Oxford, that was home. I didn't want to be the person I had left behind. I didn't want to return to the dark.

Ekram and Hassan had thrown me a goodbye party. They'd bought a goat, which had been ritually slaughtered in a neighbour's courtyard, blood drained from the neck, and they'd roasted it over an open fire. I had recited a poem I had written in Harari. Ekram gave me six hand-sewn pillowcases so I could set up my own Harari home.

My first morning back in Oxford I walked into Tesco's and burst into tears at the sight of the chickens—pasty poultry suffocated under plastic—frozen vegetables, foul-mouthed toddlers and fluorescent lights. I carried my bags full of pathetic vegetables down the street from Tesco's, passing door after closed door. Life here was all weak light behind shutters, the faint smell of cooking oil, graffiti and broken car windows and the footsteps of men making their way to the damp pub at the bottom of the hill.

Oxford rained its way into the next day, when I had an appointment at the hospital with a psychiatrist. Three days away from Ethiopia and I was resuming a weekly ritual from which I had been spared for a year. The psychiatrist excused himself shortly after I was seated, returning with two other doctors. I tried to explain to them that I was not crying because I was crazy. Anthropologists have a term for the post-fieldwork propensity to burst into tears in supermarkets: reverse culture shock. But there is no entry for this in the *DSM*.

Does it look bleak? Does it look hopeless? they asked.

"Honestly? Yes it does." It looked impossibly sad, bereft of any colour.

I was telling the truth, saying things that an anthropologist, a traveller, a dreamer, a refugee, an immigrant might understand. But these were doctors, not travellers. This was psychiatry, not poetry. I was mentally ill, not heartbroken and disoriented.

Just a week before I had been a bridesmaid at my friend Nimute's wedding. In desperation, I showed the doctors the henna on my hands, as if to prove that I had not just been to this faraway place in my imagination. I had snuck off during the third day of the wedding celebrations to spend some time with a man I wondered about marrying and raising a child with. A doctor. *He* never thought I was crazy.

These doctors didn't even allow me to return home.

That evening, I was squatting in a white hallway waiting for my medication when a Glaswegian woman behind me in line said, "Gah. How'd you burn yer hands?"

All the experiences of the past year were completely incompatible with where I found myself.

I had no visitors this time; I made no friends. I took my pills and waited out the weeks until I was free to go. I didn't know where I belonged, but I knew it wasn't there.

6

I knew what lay ahead. I had a thesis to write—an academic treatise, not a love story. My supervisor suggested a provisional structure, a way, at least, to get the treadmill started. I stepped on, dutifully plodding, each step taking me farther and farther away from an experiential sense of the place I was writing about, from the familiarity and comfort of having lived among its people, from Biscutti and Hassan, from the over-awareness of inhabiting a body.

Just a couple of months back in Oxford was all it took for me to lose sensation of my feet, my legs—they were doing the work for me, moving things along, maintaining the appearance of human functioning, of progress, while I was crumbling into dust. My body had become white particulate matter, floating in the air around people's heads. They'd breathe me in, breathe me out, unaware. I had no shape, no mass.

You can survive in this disembodied state for a time, provided you don't have to interact much with people. Graduate work at Oxford didn't require much in the way of interaction if you wanted to avoid it; there was no formal coursework, and writing a thesis is necessarily a solitary act. It doesn't really require a body beyond the occasional public appearance.

I gathered the dust into some kind of shape, like a cardboard cut-out, a single dimension, in order to give a post-fieldwork presentation in a graduate seminar on Northeast Africa. I knew I was confused, during the preparation of it, about where the emphasis of what I had to say lay. When I opened my mouth to begin, all that came out was confusion. I took another run at it, starting with something else. And then a third. And then I stopped and went silent.

My supervisor generously prompted me with a question.

I hung my head and said: I can't.

I had never experienced a moment of failure in my academic life. Ever since that turning point with David, I had been stubborn, goal-oriented, determined. But here I found myself confused and mute in front of my colleagues. Whatever was left of my cardboard exterior was burning. My face was on fire, tears cascading down over hot coals.

I pushed back my chair, excused myself. I stepped out into the grey of the Oxford winter and thought: I can never go back inside that building. It was mid-afternoon but the sky felt black. I could almost feel it resting on my shoulders. I began to walk in the direction of a park I had never felt safe walking through. I walked through that park with the sky pressing down on my back.

Ted and I usually went to the pub before having dinner at home. I can only assume that is what we did that night. Later, as he was downstairs watching TV, I was upstairs writing a note. I felt absolutely calm. I took all of my pills and some of his, and then I lay down to sleep.

I became conscious of a stream of light speeding through the dark, Ted furious, gripping the steering wheel. I woke up sometime later heaving charcoal over the side of a metal bed on wheels. This happened repeatedly throughout the night. I wept in disbelief that I was still here.

I had had enough experience of the mental health system by this point to know what and what not to say when a doctor came to do an assessment in the morning. I was not going into the psychiatric hospital again. I told the doctor that I hadn't wanted to die. That I'd just had a fight with a boyfriend.

"There are other ways of dealing with your problems," said the doctor with all the sarcastic weight he could. I was just another one of those self-absorbed borderline girls wasting everyone's time and resources. I was free to go. He gave me a prescription for a new mood stabilizer: valproic acid.

A week later I went to visit a Canadian friend who was spending her sabbatical in Oxford. I had avoided her since returning from Ethiopia. She had had her own struggles with mental health. She took one look at me and told me to get the fuck out of Oxford. "It's a swamp," she said. "It will swallow you whole. Go back to Canada and get some help."

I couldn't imagine a more humiliating defeat.

"You can finish your thesis in Toronto," Linda said, and gave me the name and number of her psychiatrist.

"You'll never finish," my supervisor said. "No one who leaves ever does."

That was all the encouragement I needed. I would finish it. Assuming I lived to do so.

7

Within a minute of meeting Linda's psychiatrist in Toronto, he asked me what was wrong with my face. I burst into tears. I hadn't realized anything was wrong with my face—it wouldn't be diagnosed as Melasma, a pigmentation change produced by estrogen and sun, until a few years later—but were we really there to talk about my face?

I asked him if he could refer me to a female psychiatrist.

"Suit yourself," he said, flipping through his Rolodex and handing me a piece of a paper.

His female colleague said nothing about my face. She asked me why I was there. I immediately told her that I didn't think I was bipolar. That I thought the psychiatrists in Oxford had been overzealous in their diagnosis because suicide was bad PR for the university.

But she wasn't prepared to question the diagnosis. She presumed the psychiatrists in Oxford knew what they were doing. She was kind enough not to say what she might have been thinking: you seem kind of crazy to me. She suggested, instead, that I find a psychotherapist if I wanted to talk about this. While she would continue to manage my medication, a therapist could help me sort out my feelings. She wrote me a prescription for Prozac and a new mood stabilizer—carbamazepine—in addition to the valproic acid I was already taking, and told me to come back in two weeks.

I made an appointment to see a therapist, a psychoanalyst, as it turned out. Freud, ids and egos, totems and taboos, these were my only associations. I sat before a tiny perfect woman and described myself as white particulate matter in the air floating around people's heads. I had no substance; I was simply being inhaled and expelled by others a thousand times in the course of every day. I had no story about how I came to be like this; just a scattering of moments. I didn't know that connecting these moments, linking them to past events, bringing forth a story would be the work of therapy. I knew just that I had tried drugs, I wasn't convinced by the diagnosis of bipolar disorder and that nothing relieved me of the wish to die.

"So why don't you stop taking the drugs?" Dr. P said.

No one had ever suggested such a thing—a steady stream of psychiatrists in England and now one in Canada had just changed my medications, upped dosages and supplemented them with even more medications. It sounded like a wild and irresponsible suggestion.

"Because," I stammered, "maybe they're the only thing I have left to hold on to."

"Why don't you hold on to me instead?"

That knocked me right in the sternum. Who has the confidence to say that? To insert oneself into the dust? To assume that kind of responsibility for anyone, particularly for a damaged stranger?

This was psychoanalysis. And it was unlike anything I had ever experienced.

I saw Dr. P three times a week. I rode my bike to her office, crossing the Bloor Viaduct: a bridge plenty high enough. Sometimes I got off my bike in the middle of the bridge on my way home. I looked down and tried to determine the best place to land. There was the Don River, but it was so shallow. There were old railway tracks, but that would be too messy. There was the multi-lane highway—too unfair to drivers. The asphalt bicycle path seemed like the best option. Presuming you fell at night, you would be unlikely to ruin any cyclist's day. But you'd need a windless night.

Having come to the same conclusion as the previous time I'd stood there, I would get back on my bike and ride home.

About a month into analysis, I put all my medication into an envelope addressed to Dr. P. I just stopped taking everything, not even taking the precaution of weaning myself off. And nothing happened. I never went back to the psychiatrist who was prescribing my medication; she didn't seem to notice. I held on to the envelope for a few more months, though. I wasn't yet prepared to give the arsenal away.

I was living in a room of a friend's house, closing my door and working on my thesis most of the hours of the day. When I wasn't working on my thesis, I was writing letters to Dr. P. Sometimes I was writing the things that I found too hard to say aloud. Other times, I was writing the story of a life I might have otherwise had.

At first that was the life of an inanimate object. A rock in a cave. It's hard to imagine that there is much to say about a rock, but I had plenty. Dr. P held that rock in her hands for some time. She had the ability to take the risk of being tender with what was hardest about me. She held that rock for long enough that it began to yield and shift shape. At some point it became a human. A baby at first, a baby in her arms on a bright and crisp fall day, leaves scattered across the ground. It was the most intimate moment I had ever shared with anyone and yet it occurred in an imaginary world.

Dr. P and I built a house together, where we lived just the two of us, and a cat. It was always a bright and crisp fall day; windows open, curtains fluttering in the wind. I was six months old sometimes, five years old, eleven. I cannot explain the process exactly, just that over the course of three years we created an alternative childhood, one that was loving and attentive. That story, the fantasy of it, couldn't replace the original, but it could exist as a counterweight: a parallel world where I could live and thrive and cultivate a different sense of self, one who wasn't crazy, one for whom depression was not the norm.

I sent Dr. P the letters I wrote to her. She didn't respond or refer to them in our sessions, but their essence was there in the room. I put the envelope full of pills in the mail to her eventually as well.

Ted responded to the letters I wrote to him. He was loving and angry in reply. We weren't ready to let go of each other. But the more time I spent in therapy, the more I began to feel that we belonged less to each other than to a common state of mind. And I wanted to be something other than depressed.

Depression blankets feelings, dulls senses, kills words. I came to know this only because once analysis began to free the feelings, out came the words. Words and feelings arrive, for me, in the same moment, as if they are one and the same.

I wrote to Dr. P every day. I also found myself writing poetry and fiction again while I was finishing my thesis. I hadn't done any creative writing since the end of high school; I'd turned my attention to academic work to the exclusion of most other things. Writing stories felt rebellious, liberating, an act of defiance against everything that was expected of me. I finished my thesis and began applying for academic jobs, but I was daydreaming about other things.

I took an administrative job at my undergraduate college in order to earn some money. I would sit and write in the college quadrangle over my lunch break, and then type my notes up at night. I had even begun sending some stories off to journals and magazines—the start of a fine career in rejection.

Sometimes I would have company in the quadrangle: a friend of one of the professors whose office was near mine. He was a disenchanted businessman who was learning Mandarin in his increasingly spare time, listening to tapes on a Walkman, repeating certain phrases aloud. He would sit down with me sometimes, ask me what I was writing, tell me about his travels.

One day, apropos of nothing, he asked me why I always looked so unhappy. I told him I felt ambivalent about an academic career, conflicted, despondent, even hostile. He asked me what I'd rather be doing, and I told him I'd rather be writing stories. He asked me what was standing in my way.

To me it seemed obvious: I couldn't just throw away something I had invested in for so long, give it all up to do something I'd never studied, embark on a profession that probably has the least chance of success or of generating income than any other profession I could possibly choose, except perhaps that of poet. I couldn't say no to a job when I had thousands of dollars in student loans to repay and absolutely nothing in the bank.

I couldn't throw everything away, most importantly, because what if I just wasn't any good?

"How would you know if you were any good?" the man learning Mandarin asked me.

I thought that if I took some time to really apply myself, to focus on writing to the exclusion of other things, I'd know either way, or the world would tell me.

"How much time would you need?" he asked.

"I don't know. Maybe six months."

"How much would it cost you to live for six months?" he asked.

I added up my rent and expenses in my head. I could live on a thousand dollars a month.

"What if I were to give you six thousand dollars?"

What? No. He couldn't be serious. But what would he expect in return?

"No strings attached," he said, as if he could read the tickertape in my head.

And he meant it. He gave me those six thousand dollars in cash the following week. The bills were in a paper box with a note reading "no strings attached."

More than the practical means, this man, a relative

stranger, gave me the shove I needed. If someone eliminates the obstacles you believe to be in front of you, then you have no choice but to try. Fail spectacularly, if you will, but try.

At the beginning of the summer, I quit my job, gave up my apartment and moved to my brother's trailer. I wasn't going to squander a second or a dollar. The trailer sat amidst two dozen others in a small park with a beautiful view of rolling sand dunes and a lake. Micah used it only on the weekends; during the week, the trailer was mine. I plugged a laptop into the outlet above the tiny stove and set myself up in a lawn chair outside. I typed while my neighbours played horseshoes. I didn't look up from my keyboard, I talked to no one.

I ate very little and I started to like the dizzy, dissociated feeling this gave me; it made me feel my body was a participant in this endeavour—quite different from the brain-in-a-box alienation I had experienced at Oxford.

Feeling the urgency, I wrote a first draft of a novel in just eight weeks. Feeling Dr. P's absence, I wrote it for her. A story of a messed-up girl who eventually finds enough companionship and sense to give her life meaning.

The experience spoiled me. Writing made it tolerable to be human in a way nothing else ever had. It gave me a place to thrive, to exorcise, to cultivate some understanding of aspects of being human that were otherwise confounding. And to put these insights into practice—to embody and enact them through character—rather than theorizing about them in an academic way. It was the perfect marriage of head and heart.

By the end of the summer, I was quite certain I wanted not just to write but to *be* a writer. Dr. P advised me to stick with the pursuit of an academic career— not unreasonable advice, and certainly the sanest course of action. But although analysis had allowed me to find a voice, I wasn't looking for reasonable advice from my analyst. I would have to leave Dr. P in order to become a writer. I would have to divorce myself from anything that might stand in my way.

part two

hatch

I

I was fulfilled by writing and relieved by publication. After my first novel was published, I was able to leave the academic world in a sensible way. I had an income from writing, a contract for another book and the prospect of a career doing something I loved, work that completely suited my personality.

I didn't have to talk. There was a text: concrete evidence that I did have something to say even if I wasn't speaking. It was grounding to have a tangible ally. And when I was speaking I didn't feel the pressure to sound smart. I could just be myself. A sense of self had emerged and developed through an intense combination of analysis and writing, a three-year period of incubation, and I found myself looking forward, excited by all that was new in my life, by all the unknown possibilities ahead.

In the fall of 2000, I was invited to attend a fundraising dinner in support of Canadian writers. I took the subway in a borrowed dress to an event where the people with money wore designer clothes and had their cars valet parked. I sat at a corporate-sponsored table, beside the host, a businesswoman. I assumed we would have little in common and would exhaust the pleasantries soon enough. Much to my surprise, we spent the whole night talking.

Anna was exceptionally generous company: smart, worldly, caustic, animated and engaged. I was surprised. Not only had she read my book, she'd made everyone at the table read it too. And she hadn't simply populated the table with begrudging colleagues; she'd carefully selected a group of interesting people from an array of backgrounds. She'd been particularly thoughtful about an evening that most would have approached as yet another obligation.

At the end of the night, she said she would love to stay in touch. Perhaps she was just being polite. We inhabited such different worlds, so little in common between them, that it was difficult to imagine the grounds for friendship. In no other context would our paths have ever crossed. But she seemed genuine, and I did, in fact, hear from her the next day. And so began a correspondence by email.

I was finishing a draft of my second novel at that time. I wanted to kill off the character of the father at the end of the story but, feeling superstitious about it, I had first hired a private detective to see whether he could locate my father, dead or alive.

For five hundred dollars I'd learned that my father was living three thousand kilometres away, in Calgary. And so, at the end of the novel, the father dies. If I hadn't known the truth, I would have felt too unsettled by mowing down my character on a lonely highway. I had taken all sorts of other imaginative liberties—filled in those missing years with fantasy, conjecture, all manner of crimes—but I could not, somehow, manage to kill him.

The last I had known of my father, he'd been squatting in the basement of a warehouse on Cherry Beach. He slept on a camp cot set up on a cement floor. There was electricity but no source of heat, several broken windows and an open channel of water running the length of the space. I visited him there only once. My brother went frequently, taking him food, and beer and clothes. He took him a pair of his own dress shoes when my father said he had a job interview. He took the shoes back when my father didn't go to the interview. An Indian giver, my father called him. Around the same time as he disowned me.

He blamed the world for betraying him. He blamed us. He disappeared altogether shortly after that.

A couple of weeks after receiving the information from the private detective, I got a phone call from my father, the first time I had heard from him in twelve years. It was creepy: he introduced himself using the name of the father in my first novel. A private detective had been sniffing around, he said. Had I hired him? And if so, why?

I told him I had simply wanted to know whether he was still alive.

But that didn't mean I had wanted to be in touch. I didn't answer his questions about whether I was married, where I lived. I vowed I would never have a listed number again.

Anna emailed to ask if anything was wrong after not having heard from me in a while. I told her something about my father. I was raw, more honest with her than the depth of our acquaintance probably warranted; she was sympathetic, attentive, more thoughtful than it warranted too.

She soon invited me for lunch downtown, in the giant tower where she worked. I was so unfamiliar with corporate geography that, rather than navigate the underground pathways, I got off the subway and made my way above ground through snow hurtling horizontally down the wind tunnels between buildings. I was wearing my most respectable and conservative black dress, but the effect was rather compromised by my boots, thick and clunky, built for weather.

She'd chosen the restaurant, high up in the tower, for the view, but all we could see out the window that day was the white heart of a storm. She ate a lobster sandwich, delicately removing the lobster from between the slices of bread, while I couldn't have eaten more than a forkful of the plate of tri-coloured fusilli in front of me because, much to my mortification, my hands were shaking.

After lunch Anna showed me the boardroom. We stood there, looking at the storm swirling outside, and she suddenly said: "I don't know if I'm shaking because I'm cold or I'm nervous."

That was all she said. That was all she needed to say. In that instant I saw beyond the tower and the title and the suit, beyond stereotypes and my own preconceptions. I saw a vulnerable and courageous heart and I was moved.

Later she would say I was the person for her. That she would wait for me for ten years.

She didn't have to.

There was something fierce and knowing about the love that grew between us, something clear and absolute and deep, and I knew, very early on, that I would love this person for the rest of my life. I hadn't known it was possible to feel conviction in love. My love for her felt thorough, pure, unassailable.

Anna told me I was easy to love.

I was quite sure I never had been. Not as a child, or an adult. Ever since my first love, David, had vanished so abruptly from my life, I'd become a disappearing act myself. I was shape-shifting, malleable, moving into the worlds of others, bringing little with me, sleeping in beds they'd slept in with previous partners, cooking with their pots and pans, enjoying the company of their friends who would come over for dinner, living in rooms painted and decorated in ways I had had no part in creating, planting nothing in their gardens, perhaps having a pot of basil by the kitchen window, that was it, a pot of basil that would last a season, if that.

I shared the cost of groceries and utilities but made no investment, took up no room, changed nothing, asked for nothing to be changed. I did not belong there. I disappeared and left no visible mark. But I left plenty of invisible ones. I was not a good person to love.

And yet, Anna believed otherwise. There was something redemptive in that. I owed too many apologies to others, some of which I would find the occasion to offer over the next few years, but the best thing I could do was love Anna well. We were a good complement to each other. Being porous allowed me to absorb some of Anna's calm and stability. And I, in turn, softened some of her harder edges. We were better for knowing and being loved by each other.

We built a life together, that loving nest I had missed in my first family, that one that gives you a sense of belonging and buffers you against the bruises of the world.

But then, Anna made being in the world easy. She took my hand early on and said: You, too, deserve to be here, participating, not just observing. Her confidence protected me, and she recast sad places in radiant light.

The first Christmas after my parents separated, my father had driven from Long Island to Buffalo to pick up my brother and me. We got to Buffalo in the back of a van without seats, a red-haired man named Bernie at the wheel. My father couldn't enter Canada for some undisclosed reason and so a stranger had driven us over the border. We waited for my father at a Howard Johnson's and then he drove us along the interstate through the night. He ordered four cups of milk at a drive-thru window, chain-smoked and told me not to fall asleep— he needed the company, he needed to stay awake.

He told me New York was the greatest city on earth, a place of giant skyscrapers and lights and art and limit-less possibility and he said we could take a helicopter ride over the city, see the sights, asked me if I would like that.

We arrived at a new housing development on Long Island in the middle of the night. There was no furniture in the townhouse, just a couple of blow-up mattresses and a table lamp on the floor. The whole place smelled of new carpet and, soon, cigarette smoke. We woke up to a grey morning. There were no trees outside and no other people living in the development from what I could gather—most of the townhouses were still under construction and I didn't see any other cars.

We went out to buy some food. All I remember him buying, though, were spices—one of every kind on the shelf—and a Christmas tree. I didn't want my father to go to the expense of a tree. We had no decorations. He bought pounds and pounds of nuts—almonds, pecans, walnuts and hazelnuts—and poured them around the base of the tree. I remember thinking: But we'll never be able to eat them all.

My father drank himself into a stupor on Christmas Eve and sat by the tree and wept. I watched him from my mattress on the floor of the living room. On Christmas morning he gave us each a canvas bag with I ♥ NY printed on it. I knew the ♥ meant love, not a word in his vocabulary. The bags were filled with freebies he'd picked up at trade shows—paper and pens and notebooks and stickers and buttons and catalogues—and cheap little puzzles and games. I wanted to be brave for my father. I tried not to and failed not to cry.

We went for a walk on a deserted beach and I found a little dead seahorse that I slipped into my pocket. We ate Christmas dinner—turkey and all the fixings—in a diner by the side of a highway.

We never saw the city, the sights. From the ground or from a helicopter.

I had fictionalized that story in my first novel. Anna was the first person I ever actually told.

I saw New York with Anna instead. She promised me it really was the greatest city on earth and set out to prove it to me. We made several trips to New York over the years. On our last, at a book launch, Anna made a passionate speech about the privilege of living with a writer. We were standing in front of a grand piano in an even grander room high above Park Avenue. I was standing on top of the world, proud partner of a proud partner in the greatest city on earth.

We got married that year in the presence of our family and friends, committing ourselves to loving and honouring and cherishing unto death. The sight of Anna's elderly and dignified Catholic father offering his blessing broke more than a few hearts. I had the feeling of a circle being made complete.

2

Almost.

Four years into our relationship, at the precise age of thirty-six years and four months, I was shocked by the strong and sudden desire to have a baby. It was a novel and completely unexpected feeling, a biological hostage-taking that I listened to but interrogated at the same time. Was it *real* desire if it was biologically driven rather than consciously determined? Was this nature's way of ensuring the survival of the species, because if we all thought about it rationally, too few of us would elect to reproduce? Was this desire a reflection of the security and comfort that Anna and I shared? Having a baby together, an extension of that love?

The answer to all those questions was yes. It no longer concerned me that I had a father who was mentally ill; I didn't worry about some biological inheritance. If you performed an autopsy on my father's life it would be a wonder if he *weren't* sick. Psychoanalysis had liberated me from fears that psychiatry had only fed.

What concerned me was the question of how I could be both a mother and a writer, both passions so all-consuming. That became the fulcrum over which the balance tipped back and forth. We would start the process of trying to get pregnant, then I would back away. Anna was patient and supportive. The desire to have a baby returned and returned again. Anna, who was six years older, understood. She'd ridden her own waves in her thirties. Now we were riding mine. Hers had subsided. Presumably mine would. By my late thirties I had felt safe in assuming they had.

We were ambitious, though, for a bit of challenge and adventure. If we weren't going to have a child, why not pursue something we had often fantasized about and move to England? We both had EU passports and family in England; more importantly, we had each other in a shared dream. And so we moved to London in the summer of 2008, full of brazen excitement. We rented out our house in Toronto, putting a question mark beside it for the time being. We had given ourselves a year in which to try to anchor ourselves.

We had a glorious and indulgent summer, with a flat

in North London, a garden in which to read the papers, a city of fabulous restaurants and markets and galleries to explore, and short trips to Dublin and Bruges.

There was the added joy for me of ample time with my cousin Tamzin. We are the daughters of two brothers—one light, one dark—and we think and feel in common ways that never require explanation.

This was the first extended period of time I had spent in Tamzin's world since she'd had children. I marvelled at her capabilities as a mother—naturally empathic but no pushover, funny and generous, frank about her own limitations and the challenges of parenting, loving and affectionate but unsentimental—absolutely solid in her role.

Her son was at school during the day and she was at home with her eighteen-month-old daughter, Lulu. I was totally smitten by this beautiful little creature. How abstract my own longing for a child had been. Apart from the long-held fantasy of adopting one little Ethiopian girl, my desire to be a mother had existed in a vacuum. Here was the day-to-day reality of life with a small child. A child to whom I was related, her mother a woman with whom I have so much in common—here was proof that people like me could be mothers.

While that love flourished, our romance with London began to wane. Three months after we arrived, Lehman Brothers declared bankruptcy, heralding a global financial crisis that was immediately palpable in London. Anna was job-hunting at the worst possible moment, months during which the words *collapse, crunch, restraint* and *austerity* dominated headlines. For my part, I couldn't even manage to persuade a newspaper editor to allow me to review a book. *We don't need your voice. We have plenty of our own.*

After the collapse we were renting a flat for double its market value. And we had signed a lease for a year. Things were suddenly looking very gloomy. We were forced to spend time apart in order to manage our responsibilities in two places, an ocean between.

Winter came. The wind rattled the single panes in our London flat and the dark came early. I recognized, far too viscerally, the greys of this place. I made the long commute to Tamzin's house and played with her baby girl.

Occasionally I looked after Lulu while Tamzin went to pick up her son. One afternoon, I was pushing Lulu in her stroller toward the tube station to meet her mother. It was a long and dodgy walk, largely unpeopled, through a sprawling council estate, and I felt a greater sense of threat than usual. I was responsible for this baby. Entirely responsible in this moment. I stuck to the road, avoiding shortcuts, crossing over whenever a man was approaching, or a large dog, or when a bend in the road obscured the view ahead.

I would kill for this child, I realized. The only other person I'd ever felt this way about was Anna. You play these games with yourself—at least I do. Would you give this person a kidney if they needed it? Your bone marrow, a lung?

I would have given Anna my heart if she'd needed it. Her life was more precious to me than my own. It's not that I still carried a suicidal impulse, that I thought my own life unworthy. It's that I am unsentimental about my own existence, a random happenstance of genetic collision. My life is not necessary, it just is. But I can cherish the life of another. I can feel almost spiritual in this regard.

I felt this way about Lulu as I pushed her along through mean streets in her stroller. I will look after your children if anything ever happens to you and their father, I would tell Tamzin later.

What were Anna and I doing? I wondered. What is it all about? If I belong anywhere, it is with Anna. I wanted my family. My Anna *and* a baby. I was forty-one years old and the desire for this was more unbridled than ever before.

I knew Anna would be a good parent. And I knew I could be a good parent with her. That we would complement each other as parents in the way we did as partners. That the best of who we were together was brave and beautiful, and that is who a child we raised together could have the potential to be. That we could lean on each other in our weakest moments. And that we could create something so much bigger than ourselves. We could love so far beyond.

It would be the most important thing we would ever do in our lives.

3

Four months later we were back in Toronto and I was pregnant. The smell of coffee lingering in my car tipped me off several days before a test could confirm it. I called Anna, who was in Chicago on a business trip. I was breathless with disbelief; she erupted with joy. She came home with a necklace she had bought that afternoon at the Chicago Art Institute. Three small stones: one tan, one silver, one grey.

We had been so lucky. The chances of conceiving at my age were slim at best. I felt the conspiracy of a huge shared and happy secret. I told Tamzin and we told Anna's sister. We would not tell our parents just yet.

I could picture cells dividing. The astonishing pace of it. At just six weeks, an ultrasound can detect a heartbeat. Life was developing so quickly on the inside, while on the outside it dragged on in a haze of fatigue.

We went to our clinic for an ultrasound in my seventh week. Anna and I held hands while the technician pointed out the heart to us. She wrote notes in a chart for the doctor. We waited for the doctor. She entered the room, her face blank.

No, I thought, no.

I remember my mother telling me that when I was born I was purple from having swallowed so much blood. The midwife whisked me off, running down the hall to have my lungs suctioned out.

My baby will be fine, my mother had said to herself.

No, I thought, no.

The heartbeat was slow, the doctor told us, slower than it should be. There was a slim chance it could rally over the next week, but. She pulled out a chart that had largely been irrelevant to me before. The rate of miscarriage in one's forties is alarming. Miscarriage was the likeliest outcome at my age. I had known this, but I took no comfort in being statistically normal. I would hold on to the idea of that slimmest chance.

A week—a week I do not remember apart from a computer screen and countless searches on the chances of a fetal heartbeat going from a trot to a gallop. And then a second ultrasound.

The doctor was a stream of words I could only partly take in. Non-viable. The heartbeat slower still, so slow it might, in fact, be mine. Dead, she meant. It might already be dead. But it was not an it, it was our son. I knew it would be a boy. We had made lists of names, but the one that came to mind in that moment was Hamish. I was supposed to be at home with Hamish in the spring, not worrying about my career for two years. I had pictured him toddling unsteadily down our flagstone path, Anna arriving home from work.

If he was not dead, he soon would be. I had a choice between allowing the miscarriage to occur in its own time, after which a D & C might still be necessary, or taking this medication—the doctor was already writing the scrip—and expediting the process.

I could not bear the thought of my body being the home to something dead or nearly so. Of waiting days, perhaps weeks, for it to leave me. Of prolonging the grief. I took the prescription from the doctor's hands.

She led us to a room for some privacy. It was over. Hamish would not be born. We would not be his parents. I was wearing a necklace with three small stones.

4

I had, at least, been able to get pregnant. There was hope in that. But I didn't have much time to waste. As soon as I could, I started trying to conceive again. Three months later, I was pregnant once more. Anna gave me flowers this time, withholding some enthusiasm, unwilling perhaps to invest too early and in something so uncertain.

Everything was different this time round. I felt no sense of joy emanating from either of us. I was more fatalistic about this pregnancy, less precious. A piece of brie wasn't going to kill a fetus. There were bigger determinants at work, things beyond my control. I had no sense of this fetus as a person, a boy or girl, no image of him or her as a toddler. I was resigned to fate. If this resulted in another miscarriage, I wouldn't risk a third.

Those first eight weeks were a strange period of suspension. Anna and I were muted with each other, cautious around this pregnancy. We were waiting for that first ultrasound, breaths held. We had sold our house, furthermore, failing to find another before winter set in. It was January, and in this brittle season of hard ground but little snow, we were renting a house belonging to friends who were away on sabbatical for the term. All our belongings were in storage, and would remain so until we found something in the surge of new listings that would arrive with spring.

There was so much uncertainty about the future— I could only hold on to the certainty of us, of our commitment to each other. Life is long: we will be many things in the course of it. I knew we could be all those things, even the most painful, together.

Anna held my hand through the first ultrasound. I saw the rapid flutter of a heartbeat. I paid attention to numbers that had meant nothing last time round. I'd done my research. This one was a galloper. The doctor confirmed it. I was overjoyed and hugged her; Anna did as well. This was a promising sign, the good start we'd been denied the first time. The suspense wasn't over— the chances of losing a pregnancy in the first trimester at my age are two out of three—but we were further ahead than we had been six months before. If all continued to go well, we would be three by next September. That most ordinary of things. A family.

In the meantime, I had a novel to finish. It was at the proofreading stage, but I was finding it difficult to concentrate. The story is set in Vietnam, which Anna and I had visited twice in 2007. We first went to the country on holiday. We returned to Hanoi later that year so that I could conduct some research for the novel that had been inspired by the first trip. I wondered whether we'd have such adventures with a baby, whether the world would suddenly feel very small, whether I'd ever again have the time to write a novel. I'd put off having a baby this long in large part because of such concerns, but they no longer seemed to matter.

I was looking forward to this shift in focus, but for the time being, I was exhausted. Exhausted and lonely with just my manuscript for company in this big house in winter, Anna at work, all our belongings in storage, this uncertainty in my belly, someone else's cat. And it was so grey out there. It had been this bitter grey for months.

Fortunately we had a week of holiday in the sun to look forward to. In two days we'd be going to the Caribbean with Anna's sister and brother-in-law. Later in the day I unearthed our suitcases and some of our summer clothes. I shopped for groceries and cooked in anticipation of Anna coming home. I always looked forward to her company and conversation at the end of the day. Anna's return the return of the world.

That night, shortly after Anna came home from work, a friend emailed each of us to ask if we wanted to join her for her daughter's hockey practice. It was a dark, cold night in late January and I was simply too exhausted to consider it. The prospect held no appeal for me, and wouldn't normally for Anna either, so I was surprised, even hurt, when she said yes.

I went to bed, tried to sleep in the bedroom on the top storey. The house was massive—a family home without a family. The bedroom was lonely and far from earth, so high that it sat just above the naked treetops. I tried to sleep while Anna was out but I just couldn't stop crying. I was overcome with a deep, dark sense that I had just been abandoned.

I went downstairs and waited in the kitchen in my pyjamas. As soon as Anna got home I asked her what was going on. I was shaking, my voice unfamiliar. The question came from some primal place I had never before visited with Anna. A place of terrible fear. I had no idea what might come next, of what kind of answer might follow this kind of question. If the question felt this bad though, surely the answer couldn't be good.

I don't remember if she was still wearing her coat or sitting down or standing up. I do know that there was no hesitation on her part when she told me that she wasn't happy. She had lost her passion for me and that had eroded her love for me.

I pleaded with her to go to couples counselling. She said there was nothing to fix.

She had made a decision. Our relationship was over. A fait accompli.

"Life changes in the instant. You sit down to dinner and life as you know it ends." We'd both read *The Year of Magical Thinking*, Joan Didion's memoir of the loss of her husband. We'd been to New York and seen Vanessa Redgrave in its adaptation for the stage. Anna had been far more moved by Didion's meditation on loss. People die, I had thought at the time. What privileges your story above others?

Perhaps you cannot understand until the instant is upon you. *This* was the instant. "The ordinary instant." Mine. The most devastating moment of my life. Everything I trusted in had been obliterated, including me, my entire being carved out with a knife. And in that hollow was the seed of a person I was supposed to nurture. I was supposed to grow a person. When I was no longer a person.

Anna left for St. Barts. I moved to the bed upstairs. I couldn't sleep for all my first-trimester exhaustion. I barely ate. My hands shook. I had this bodily terror that some fatal blow was going to come at me from some unanticipated direction. I have never been more terrified in my life. I kept my eyes wide open, but took in nothing. When I did sleep I had violent nightmares. I wasn't human anymore; I had become animal, alert to the scent of danger all around me.

My cheeks were hot and wet with tears every time I woke up.

One morning, it wasn't tears but blood on my hands. I looked at the pillow. The pillow was saturated in red. I threw back the sheet. No blood. I worried about the blood ruining the pillowcase, the pillow, neither of which was mine. I dripped blood into the bathroom, splattering its white tiles. I worried about staining the tiles. I got on my knees to wipe up the blood but it just kept on coming, pouring out of my head. My blood pressure plummeted; I had to pull myself up holding on to the vanity. My vision was pixilated: yellow stars against a dark grey sky.

The day Anna came home from holiday I shopped for her favourite foods so that there was something for her to eat. Because this couldn't really be happening. Of all the potential futures, this was not one I had ever imagined.

We had overcome so many obstacles in order to have that most ordinary of things. Everything was in place for us to be a tidy nuclear family.

But suddenly there would be no *us*.

There would be no family.

There would just be me, alone.

Hatching an egg

without

a nest.

5

There was no escape. I couldn't eat much or sleep. I couldn't read, write, watch TV, listen to music. I couldn't face or find language. I couldn't think in anything but tortured circles. This couldn't be happening. She'd be back; she wouldn't do this, she couldn't. And yet Anna had been nothing but resolute. She had moved out the day after returning from holiday. There had been no unravelling or dissolution. No expressions of love or doubt or regret. No last gasps.

I fought off thoughts of the bridge that certainly was high enough, of overcoming the pain of this with the pain of something else. But there was nothing I could do to relieve myself of it, not even the momentary transcendence of getting drunk. A little heart was beating inside me. A life growing bigger every day. I was trapped in this grieving and unknown body. And now a baby was trapped here too.

The only person I could really talk to was Tamzin. She called me every single day, as she would for months. It was late in her world, her kids in bed, and she called and just listened to me cry.

I made an appointment to see the social worker we had visited for a mandatory consultation when we began trying to conceive. I could barely get the words out through the wall of tears. I was tormented by the thought that my pain might be deforming what I was carrying, destroying it in some way. I was terrified to give birth to a baby that I had ruined. I needed to know whether I should end my pregnancy. But I was afraid that if I was no longer carrying a baby, I would lose any will to live. There would be nothing left to hold on to.

I was trapped in this spiralling eddy. I needed a professional opinion. I tried to put all this into plain words.

It's a parasite, the social worker reassured me. All it needs is your blood.

6

Our friends would soon be back from sabbatical and reoccupying their house. There was a separate apartment in the basement and they told me I could stay there for as long as I wanted. It was kind and generous of them, but I couldn't imagine another temporary situation, especially one where I was pregnant and alone in someone's basement. Pride was also preventing me from returning to my mother's house.

I needed somewhere to live. I needed a structure around me. I needed to act quickly. I needed to buy a house that closed in a matter of weeks.

In the dirty grey middle of winter, and in an inflated market, my real estate agent took me into the foyer of yet another dark, overpriced house in need of gutting. He tried to sell me on the possibilities he envisioned, and I burst into tears at the prospect of the work and the expense. I couldn't even see straight. He put a box of tissues on top of the parking brake in his car and we carried on.

We soon went east, over the river. I had lived in this end of the city years before. Running through it is a humble stretch of Vietnamese bakeries and restaurants where I'd been consuming bánh mì and pho for years. I put in an offer on the first house I saw—a semi-detached Victorian with a good feel. The house was in need of quite a lot of work, but I could see its potential. A child lived there; there was a crib in the back bedroom. A child belonged in this house.

There was an intense bidding war that I fought because I needed to land somewhere I'd feel safe and comfortable as a single mother. I needed this house. We would live in this house and we would eat bánh mì and pho. At least this much I knew.

I had two more months of winter to spend in the big lonely house. Afraid of the isolation of the bedroom, I slept on the couch downstairs. I'd lost ten pounds, one for each week of my pregnancy, but my belly was bloated and hard. Alice, the ancient cat in the house, would knead the bump before settling down to lie on my chest. She held on during the waves of sobbing, claws dug in for the ride.

I hated the weekends most of all. I dreaded them. I had to distract myself with something other than the depressing task of gathering papers for the family lawyer I had engaged. I had to get out of this house. My literary agent suggested meeting in New York. I can do this, I thought. I have reasons for being in New York that have nothing to do with Anna.

I got pulled aside for a manual body search as I was boarding the plane. I told the official I was pregnant, feeling protective of my stomach. It was the first time I'd told a stranger. I felt an embarrassed rush of pride as I said it.

It was hard enough carrying around the knowledge that I was pregnant during the first trimester, but this was part of the story of Anna's departure that I had not been able to share. Mutual friends knew Anna had left me, but not that I was pregnant. The risk of my miscarrying during those early weeks was just too high; sharing news that could end in another tragedy, heaping one loss on top of another, was too much to consider.

It was easier, in fact, to tell a stranger.

Two weeks after going to New York, I went to Boston alone. It was my birthday: forty-two. As long as I could keep moving, I knew I was still alive. I knew two people in Boston, neither of them well. I told both of them that I was pregnant. I bought a stretchy tie-dyed dress at

American Apparel to accommodate the bump. It was no longer invisible to everyone but me.

I took a taxi home from the airport. The sun was shining, it was suddenly spring, and I was hungry. I got out of the taxi on a busy street and went into a restaurant. I ordered a lot of food. In that moment I suddenly overcame a lifetime of being self-conscious about eating on my own in public. Because I wasn't, in fact, on my own.

7

At twelve weeks, my best friend, Vibika, accompanied me to an obligatory genetic counselling appointment. We had known each other, by this point, for thirty-eight years. When we were four years old, my family moved in next door to hers. We had come from England. They had come from Italy by way of the U.S. the year before. Vibika's father built a playhouse in their backyard, a stage in their basement. We were ponies and prisoners, ballet dancers and the cast of *Jesus Christ Superstar*. We charged admission to our largely unscripted performances and bought Doritos and Cokes and Mars Bars with the profits. We ran around barefoot and shirtless in the rain banging milk jugs together. Even our cats were friends.

Our fun took place only at Vibika's house, though. She and her sister were afraid of my father.

After five years of best-friendship, things in our worlds began to wobble. First, Vibika's parents split up. Less than a year later, so did mine. Hard to believe now, but ours were the only two divorced families I knew. We were ten, and school and our friends assumed more importance, as they would have anyway, but the need for a world beyond was amplified by the destabilizing changes at home.

Vibika's mother moved away on something of a spiritual quest. Ara came to live with us, but two years later he was gone. Then my brother went to live with my father. And Vibika's mother developed cancer. She died in her early forties. Micah came back home after two years with my father and promptly dropped out of school. A year later, my father disappeared from our lives altogether, and sometime after that my mother and Vibika's father both remarried. Despite our best efforts, they did not marry each other.

We've remained friends, growing even closer over the years. Ours is perhaps the longest and most uncomplicated relationship either of us will ever have.

I asked Vibika to come to the appointment because I couldn't bear the thought of being there alone in a room full of nervously happy couples. I needed to be there with someone who loved me.

We were seated in a room with five couples, everyone over thirty-five. This was not a celebration: the nurse leading the presentation was all doom and gloom. It was not enough that we'd managed to hold on to our pregnancies through the first trimester. Our risks for chromosomal abnormalities were daunting. Ninety per cent of a forty-year-old's eggs are damaged in some way.

We watched an ancient video where a woman gets the happy news of a positive pregnancy over the phone and calls her husband at work. A month later she is wearing a muumuu, agonizing over whether to have amniocentesis. Vibika, a television producer, couldn't refrain from remarking on the crappy production values. Neither of us could get over the muumuu. Our laughter was disruptive. I realized the other people in the room must have assumed we were a couple. When I whispered this to Vibika, she said she couldn't be more proud.

The first test revealed minimal risk for Down's and other chromosomal abnormalities. I felt proud of my baby, my little egg. He was stronger than me. He had a will to survive beyond my own.

Vibika accompanied me to the later appointment for amniocentesis. She held my hand while that long needle went straight into my belly. The Saudi doctor told me my little egg was a girl. I asked her in Arabic whether she was sure. I had studied Arabic for years, but it was Ara who taught me the word for penis. The things that stay with us. The places they prove handy.

I didn't relay the results of the amniocentesis to

Anna. My body, my business, I told myself, although I knew it was much more complicated than that.

I wouldn't be able to keep her at such a distance. The first thing my lawyer told me was that Anna had rights and responsibilities where this child was concerned. We'd conceived her together, in some respect, after all. Canadian law doesn't care about the gender or biological ties of the parents to the child or how conception took place. It endorses the idea of two parents for the well-being of the child. Anna had rights if she wanted them, responsibilities whether she wanted them or not.

But I had no idea what *I* wanted. I was paralyzed— all flaming feeling, no insight or calm or clarity. I was crying all the time, I was angry and afraid, I couldn't write, and all I wanted was for Anna to come home, to say she had made a tragic mistake, to be the family we were supposed to be. I couldn't conceive of any other configuration. No fantasy replaced the original—the only—idea. I didn't want anything else. I had certainly never wanted to be a single parent.

Vibika encouraged me to name the egg. She was trying to make her real, shift my attention, encourage the growth of a relationship between us. She was right to. Despite the growing evidence of the egg's presence, I had remained in a state of largely suspended disbelief. I picked something without much thought or reason; a name that must have been in the air. The egg was now a girl with a pretty name.

8

The day of my move, an old Greek man sweeping the sidewalk in front of my new house waved hello and barked: "You the pregnant lady?"

I nodded, feeling rather exposed.

"Everything will be okay," said the man, nodding his head and saluting me.

I wanted, so desperately, to believe him.

The week before Anna had announced it was over, a man had come to the door selling fish. Boxes of beautiful line-caught fish. I'd been thinking about spring, of the barbecues we would have with our friends once the weather got warmer. The house we had rented was an ideal place to entertain; it had a beautiful kitchen overlooking an architectural wonder of a backyard.

I spent a fortune on a bag of line-caught sea bass fillets. I was planning into the future, our spring and summer ahead. I was thinking well beyond, in fact. I imagined life, all of it—the pleasure and pain, the indignity and the glory of it—shared.

After Anna left, I couldn't bear to see those fish in the freezer. I put the box in the freezer in the apartment in the basement. I could have thrown them out; I probably should have. If I were writing a novel or a screenplay, I would have me cooking all those fish and stuffing myself full of them in one sitting. And not tasting a thing. A tragicomedy.

In real life I just put them out of sight. I left them behind, those hundreds of dollars' worth of fish, when I moved out that morning. I couldn't bring myself to tell my friends about the fish in their freezer. I never told anyone. The humiliation was too great. The naivety and blind optimism of the purchase.

Everything Anna and I owned was now coming out of storage, the whole psychological mess of it coming here to my new house to be sorted through. Nine years of shared possessions, every single one of them with a story: worst of all, the photo albums.

It would have been easier to just leave it all in a storage locker. Lives have been abandoned to storage lockers before. Instead, I carted all these painful mementoes of the past decade into a house that was more rundown than I remembered. It was dingy and depressing, in fact.

Perhaps most houses feel like this when you move into them: stripped of furniture, the holes in the walls, the dust that hid behind furniture, the bare bulbs. All the things you failed to notice before made starkly obvious—the slope and creak of the floors, the vents that connect rooms, carrying sound, the flock wallpaper on the ceiling that has simply been painted over, the bubbling to the walls that reveals the framing of the lathe and plaster, the lack of closets.

The next night, while I was alone with my boxes, one of my neighbours started a bonfire in his backyard. He was feeding two-by-fours into the fire. Sparks were flying upward into the trees. He pulled a karaoke machine on a dolly into his yard and his teenage kids cranked up the volume and played the bongos until midnight. It was a Sunday night in April, for Christ's sake.

On Monday morning a contractor arrived with his crew to tear out my kitchen. An electrician started in on the job of pulling out all the old knob-and-tube wiring, which needed replacing. I hadn't even been in this house for forty-eight hours and already it was being dismantled around me. There was suddenly no kitchen. In fact, the entire back wall of the house was gone, replaced by a tarp—a little too reminiscent of my father's farmhouse—and the rains of April were lashing down. There were holes in every other wall and ceiling. Plaster was falling down and drywall dust filled the air. Addressing one problem revealed several others—termites and mould and damp.

I was confined to a single habitable room and living on Vietnamese takeout. The heating ducts were being rerouted when the temperature suddenly dropped, so I pulled my mattress into the hallway, wedging it between the banister and the wall, and slept behind the plastic sheet sealing off the front room of the house.

This was where I was lying when my baby started to make her presence known, startling me with the lightest of touches, as if she was swiping a paintbrush across the inside my belly. She was real. *This* was real. What the fuck was I doing? This was no way for us to live. The next day, I packed up my shame, stubbornness, reluctance, and went to stay at my mother and stepfather's house.

The last time I had stayed there for any length of time was in the first few weeks after I'd returned from England fourteen years ago. I was profoundly depressed then, though doing my best not to show it. There was a surreality to being back in that house, a collapse in time—as if I had never been married, as if I had never been happy—as if I was, in fact, just fourteen, fourteen and pregnant, single and ashamed and afraid and depressed and sleeping in the bed I had always slept in, my stepfather cooking dinner every night.

I returned to the east end every day in order to remind myself this was not the case, that I was an adult, owner of a house currently under renovation, not an adolescent cliché. I had lights and furniture and appliances and cabinetry to buy. I made sixteen trips to Ikea in two months. When the electrical work was done, I moved back into my house so that I could sand and sweep and paint.

It would have been nice—more than nice—if someone had been doing this with me. Nice, too, if someone had made me a cup of tea, made a midnight run for Swiss cheese or cooked me lentils, the two things I craved. It would have been nice to have been taken out for dinner, to have had someone help take out the garbage, clean the house, share the changes in my body, talk to my belly, feel her move, notice her hiccup, accompany me to prenatal classes, tell me I was beautiful, keep me company during sleepless nights, prop me up with pillows, love me and tell me so, ask me about my fears, reassure me that everything would be okay, have doubts with, be scared with, be reassured by me, a me made strong by this belly. It would have been so much more than nice.

A pregnant body is an animal body, a body within a body, a secrets-in-public body, a sexy body, a threatening body, a woman's body, a fighting, growing body, an alien and impossible body. It is impossible not to notice, and yet I was completely unseen by the person I loved, the only person who really mattered.

I was feeling isolated and invisible, yet suddenly burning with a second-trimester desire that no one had ever warned me about. Not *What to Expect When You're Expecting*, not my midwife, not Tamzin, certainly not my mother and none of my few friends who'd had children. Perhaps it was supposed to be a shared secret, some primal bonding between you and the person with whom you had conceived while the fetus was becoming a child. Perhaps this was the closest you could get to sharing a pregnancy.

I shamelessly begged someone I'd always had a thing for to fuck me. That someone did me the honour of obliging. It was the roughest and most powerful sex of my life: fearless and life giving. It restored life to a body creating a body. I existed, for a brief moment, as a pregnant woman in intimate relationship to another person. And then I shut down, retreating inward. My baby was taking over; she felt bigger than me now. I had to marshal all my strength in order to take care of her.

9

A friend introduced me to a pregnant woman in my new neighbourhood—a doctor who had chosen to have a baby on her own. She had prepared a spreadsheet of things that needed to be done in the countdown to her baby's arrival. I was thoroughly intimidated by her enthusiasm and togetherness; I was miserable and completely unprepared. I suppose there's a burden of expected cheerfulness imposed on every pregnant woman, but I was utterly incapable of even faking it.

The egg, meanwhile, dropped her paintbrush for some more vigorous activity. I watched with equal parts fascination and horror as my stomach turned into a wave. She was swimming, and every time she reached the end of the pool she did that flip turn that I had never mastered. She was so robust, such a kicker, that if she was still for any length of time, I worried. Rather than calling the midwife, I got into the bath. She didn't respond to music or a cup of juice, but she liked the sound of running water. I ran the hot tap until it was cold.

I will teach her how to swim. It was my first independent thought of who we would be to each other in the real world, in the world outside my body.

I signed us up for aquafit and began to search for a prenatal class for single women. I found only one in the city that wasn't for teenagers, but it welcomed only women who were single by choice, not as a consequence of death or divorce. Because this was supposed to be a time of celebration. There's no place for your grief and loneliness here!

Vibika and another friend, Heidi, agreed to accompany me to the prenatal classes offered at my midwifery clinic. Surely there would be feminists and lesbians and unmarrieds and oddballs in a class offered by a midwifery clinic. But midwifery had perhaps become more mainstream than I had realized: the other women in the class all came accompanied by largely silent husbands.

The women were impatient with the instructor's agenda, and right away they hijacked it with detailed questions about delivery—whether they could have a water birth, whether there were dimmers in the delivery rooms, whether they could play music, whether they could eat during labour. They were decorating the rooms for themselves, programming their playlists, hoping to create the perfect environment for this life-altering moment.

During the break they compared notes on strollers and car seats. One woman said her husband didn't want her driving the Volvo anymore because of the possibility of the airbags inflating and knocking her in the stomach. I actually rolled my eyes.

And then I started crying. I had spent the day on a ladder priming an oil-painted ceiling. I hated these women for their petty preoccupations. I hated these women because I should have been one of them. I hated them most of all for being loved.

I was a toxic cloud. For their sake and my own, I couldn't go back into that room.

Vibika instead hired a private instructor to guide us through three classes at my house. I kept Vibika and Heidi's glasses topped up with wine, while we played with a doll and a plastic uterus. We contemplated the impossibility of getting *that* through *that*. I joked with Vibika that she might have to massage my perineum. "Sure," she said. "What is it?"

10

By mid-June I was beginning to feel the strain of my pregnancy—a compressed sciatic nerve and an umbilical hernia. And then the basement flooded. I was lucky a friend was over for dinner the night it happened. I knelt down in a puddle in the basement among all the sodden boxes of books I had yet to unpack. The water was a foot deep where the concrete floor sloped toward the door. My friend bailed water out the basement door by the bucketful. The boxes were too big and heavy for me to shift. I broke down, feeling defeated and sorry for myself. I started tearing into the boxes and hurling damaged books at the wall.

I was suddenly conscious of, then self-conscious about, the drama. I saw myself in a scene from a movie.

And then I saw my mother, years ago, kneeling beside the bathtub, pliers in hand, crying.

I was standing behind her, eleven years old. "What's the matter?" I asked, and not kindly.

"I can't turn it," she said. She was trying to replace a washer, fix a persistent drip.

I still didn't understand why this would be cause for tears. I didn't understand why a drip was such a problem, why it mattered.

I remember the story of my birth: me, a purple baby in an incubator, my mother in a ward with thirty other women and their newborns, one bath shared between them all. For ten days. She couldn't stand the surroundings and she certainly couldn't stomach the food. My father had felt helpless and asked what he could bring. I'd love a piece of chicken, she said, imagining thin white slices of breast meat. He roasted a whole chicken and brought it to her the next day in a brown paper bag. It's the closest she's ever come to telling me anything like a love story between them.

She took one look at the congealed grease on that brown paper and told him he'd have to take it away.

A metaphor, perhaps. For years, she was a single mother doing her best to make us a good home. There was no one to help change a washer. She did not spare me: when I was eighteen she told me straight out that we are all alone in the world. For a time, I hadn't believed her.

I had become my mother, bucket in hand instead of pliers.

Stand up, I willed myself. Stand. The fuck. Up.

A week later, Anna and I met with our lawyers to negotiate the details of our separation. It was the same week that would have seen us celebrating our fourth wedding anniversary. I was seven months pregnant, not sleeping, anxious as hell.

She wanted to co-parent. She said this plainly, as did her lawyer.

It had been easy, in her absence, in the virtual silence between us those past few months, to tell myself she didn't want anything to do with the baby. Yet there she was, stating plainly that she did.

But we were not separate, this baby and I: we were one. The only way this could make sense to me was if she were coming home.

We settled things financially and agreed to go and see a parenting mediator.

Anna would find her way. I just had to be patient. I had to show her that I was competent and strong. I could do this. I could be the rock for us all.

11

I suddenly heard from my brother, whom I hadn't heard from in years. He sent a text: "Holy shit, Min, you're having a baby! That's fucking awesome!"

I suppose everyone in my family was incredulous. Perhaps my mother recognized the unlikelihood early on; she never exerted any pressure, never even expressed a desire for grandchildren. And yet, when I did become pregnant, she began to unearth clothes, a bassinet, a hairbrush, blankets, cups, bowls and spoons—things she'd carried across an ocean and held on to for more than forty years.

Micah and I had never talked about having kids. But then we hadn't really talked as adults.

Fourteen summers before, when I gave up my apartment in the city and took up residence in my brother's trailer, the bond between us, a bond I had believed to be unbreakable, had been shattered.

One weekend my brother came up with his then girlfriend, a troubled, quiet girl with white face paint and pierced black lips. My brother is a canvas of tattoos—her look was not unfamiliar in his world, but out there, in the woods, it was startling. She looked like she'd never seen the sun, and yet they spent the weekends engaged in the all-Canadian summer pastimes of boating, fishing, jet skiing, barbecuing large slabs of meat and drinking beer.

He went off one night to fix a pipe in a neighbouring trailer, and I was forced to be polite and make conversation with the girlfriend. She opened up a bit, talking about her family. An hour later Micah came home, found us talking in the trailer and asked us what the fuck we were up to. He was so angry his hands were shaking. I'd never seen him like this and it scared me. I retreated to the tent but couldn't shut out the sounds of their fighting.

It was the middle of the night when I woke up startled, a flashlight shining in my face. My brother started ranting, shouting profanities so extreme I can't repeat them to this day. I started to cry. I didn't understand what I had done wrong. For fuck's sake—he'd left me with the damaged goth girl, I'd just been doing my best to find some point of connection.

He growled and barked at me. Seeing me scared, huddling inside the tent, only fuelled him. I was thirteen years old again, night had fallen. I found myself shrinking in the corner of my brother's tent.

But wait—I wasn't thirteen anymore. I tried to push past him to get out, but he blocked me. He abruptly left, but moved his truck so that it hemmed in the tent and my car. I was trapped for the night. I left early the next day. I returned to the trailer on Monday morning. I stayed during the week and slept in my car on the weekends. I had nowhere else to go.

We hadn't spent time together as a family since; not a Christmas dinner in fourteen years. I never did get an explanation or an apology. Several years after this incident, he started calling me in the middle of the night to tell me he didn't want me to be afraid of him anymore. I stopped picking up the phone. A few years later I learned he had a serious drug problem. That explained his rage and paranoia, but it did not absolve him. It made me feel so sad for the lovely boy he had once been, so guilty that I should have survived the mess of my father where he had not. But I was no less afraid of him.

Hence my total surprise at this text. My situation had moved him to make contact. He told me he'd been clean for a year and a half and he asked if there was anything he could do to help. He had stepped up just when I needed him most. A giant wave of forgiveness swept over the past fourteen years.

"Build me a deck?" I said, my nesting instinct now extending to the world outside.

"You got it," he replied.

It took him a month to turn up, but when he did, he arrived with tools in hand, ready to work. I heaved the bulk of myself into the cabin of his big stencilled pickup with its overflowing ashtray, sagging seats, gun rack and littered floor, and he flipped open the engine lid to connect the battery to start the truck, jerked it into neutral (which is actually first), cranked the heavy metal, rolled the windows down for some relief in the stifling heat and drove us to the lumber yard, chain-smoking the whole way.

This was not how I pictured spending the last week of my pregnancy. It was not, I imagined, where a woman in her last week of pregnancy should be.

And yet, I soon had a beautiful cedar deck under way as well as plans for a flower bed and a water feature. More importantly, I had a brother for the first time in years.

12

My house was finally in order. There were newly painted rooms upstairs: an office and two bedrooms. One of those was for my baby and me, one of them for a nanny.

A nanny had never occurred to me before an acquaintance, a writer himself, had raised the issue a few months earlier. He and his wife had employed a nanny for years. As he reminded me, I had a book to launch that September, just a few weeks after I would give birth, followed by a book tour. How was I going to do all that on my own?

Considering a nanny was possible only because Anna and I had agreed to this in our legal negotiations.

I was fortunate in this regard, at least; I wouldn't have had the same choices otherwise.

Tita, a beautiful twenty-nine-year-old Filipina, arrived a week before my due date, while my brother was finishing work outdoors. She brought very little with her, all of it contained in a knapsack.

I'd never employed anyone before. The prospect made me nervous; I didn't know how to be, how to ask someone to do something for me, how to assume any authority. I wanted her to feel at home. I'd painted her room a buttery white, put a lock on the door, bought an armoire and a night table and a chest of drawers and a television and a DVD player for her room. I'd cleared off a shelf in the bathroom cupboard for her, but she didn't use it. She didn't leave her shoes on the shoe rack either, or hang her jacket in the front hall.

She was quiet. She was thoughtful and diligent. Perhaps she was wondering what she had just signed up for. I had been crying solidly for eight months; the tears didn't stop with Tita's arrival.

After meeting a succession of my male friends, Tita asked me straight out which one the father was. "Well," I hesitated, "it's complicated." Anna's name and mine were on her employment contract, but I'd avoided giving Tita the explicit details of the situation. I had assumed a certain conservatism based on religion and culture, and I feared she would judge me and flee before she even knew me. It was time for the facts.

"Why didn't you tell me?" she almost shouted. "I may have bad English but I have a very open mind!"

I liked her spirit. And it hadn't taken long to see evidence of it. A baby is a baby, however it is conceived, and it was the baby that would define our relationship to each other.

The only problem was that the baby was refusing to come out. My due date had passed. A week, ten days. It was nearing the middle of September. I had been pregnant every day of 2010. I would have to forgo breathing if she insisted on taking up any more room.

I'd been eating Thai soups and Pakistani curries, all manner of spicy food in the hopes of getting things moving. I'd had acupuncture and massage, eaten my weight in pineapple (prostaglandins, apparently), run up and down the stairs, done all the things people say you might to bring on labour, with the exception of having vigorous, penetrative sex. It just didn't seem like the right moment to be recruiting a stranger into the mix.

Ten days past my due date, feeling restless and housebound, I went to a Saturday farmers' market with a friend. It was a beautiful day—clear blue sky relieved of summer's humidity, an exciting sense of back-to-school in the air. As we entered the market, we were both immediately drawn to a brown-skinned man with magnetic blue eyes and snow-white hair standing alone at a stall past the late-summer blueberries and tomatoes.

He was selling tea, from his home—Ceylon, he said, not Sri Lanka. After a brief conversation about his hillside plantation, my friend bought some exorbitantly priced leaves simply because of the man's beauty. The man then held out a small tinfoil square of tea leaves for me, saying: "This will help bring on your labour."

I was grateful to him for recognizing the overdueness of the situation and for his kind gesture of help. At that point I would have eaten a hornets' nest if someone suggested it. "I'll name my child after you if it works," I said. He told me his name was Norbert. It was lucky I was having a girl.

That night, I sat on the couch and watched the first half of season 1 of *True Blood*. The blood and sex of it struck me as entirely appropriate. I drank a cup of this man's induction tea. It was probably coincidental, but five hours later the contractions started.

They didn't feel urgent. I didn't call anyone. I spent the night alone because I wanted to be alone with my imminent daughter. I felt as if I hadn't yet just been still with her. Talked enough to her. Spent enough time with her. So much of me had been disengaged from this pregnancy, necrotized by grief, trying to distract myself by keeping occupied. But suddenly a baby was about to be born.

I found myself crying and apologizing for all that was not as I wished it to be for her. I had wept for hours every single day of this pregnancy. I didn't want her to have a sad mother, a single mother, an old mother. I didn't want to be sad, single and old. And yet.

On Sunday morning, Vibika and Heidi said goodbye to their men and their dogs and came over with wine and chips. We got through the rest of season 1, pausing for contractions, and a good way into season 2. Vibika and Heidi took turns napping. Tita brought us endless cups of tea.

Vibika drove me across town twice to the midwifery clinic for fetal heart monitoring. I had never experienced anything comparable to the pain of bouncing over streetcar tracks while having contractions, my fingernails embedded in the roof of a VW Bug.

The baby was fine, but we were all exhausted. By Tuesday afternoon we gave up and went to the hospital. Vibika pushed me down the hall in a wheelchair and into an elevator. I felt both giant and tiny, completely exposed in my nightgown, all these people upright and moving intact, their bodies familiar to them, doing predictable things.

I was relieved to see the midwife. She ushered us straight into the delivery room even though we had hours to go. After more than sixty hours in labour, I was still only five centimetres dilated.

My mother arrived after work. I was relieved to see her as well. She was the only one in this room who had given birth before. They didn't have epidurals in her day, but although I'm not too proud for them, I lean toward less intervention rather than more. I had had no way of imagining the pain or what I might be capable of withstanding; I had left it open to consider the options in the moment, aware that there can be a moment too late. I realized, though, that after all this time in labour I was just not going to have any strength left for the main event. I think this was what I told my midwife, though Vibika would later tell me I wasn't quite so polite.

An anaesthetist came to administer an epidural. A second anaesthetist repeated the process a couple of hours later, when the first epidural refused to take. The midwife broke my water with something that looked like a knitting needle. Nothing was like it is in the movies. The contractions began to slow down because of the epidural. The midwife inserted an IV into my arm and began to administer oxytocin. By this point, I was disappointed in myself. I hadn't wanted this much intervention. A catheter was the final insult.

The moment for pushing had finally arrived. My mother made no move to leave as we'd both expected she would. I asked her if she was okay, if she really wanted to stay. Her bottom lip trembled; she couldn't speak. I felt closer to her in this moment than I had ever felt or will likely ever feel again. She held my head, curved it upright. She was the top of the C, Vibika and Heidi, with a leg each, the bottom.

I lost all sense of time and place. Voices became disembodied, and lights faded in and out as if I was underwater. I didn't know if this was pain. This was determination in the face of impossibility. I heard the baby's heartbeat underwater. And then there was a baby. There was a baby in my arms. Bloody and bruise-lipped with black hair. Mine.

Is it real? I asked Vibika. Is it real? I repeated this over and over until I realized I was repeating it over and over.

Yes, she's real, Vibika kept saying. *She.*

But it didn't feel real. Where was the overwhelming swell of love I'd been promised I would feel in this instant? Why didn't I feel anything other than shock? And where was everyone going? Their work done, they were all quickly fading away. But wait—I felt such panic. You cannot go: this is where the real work begins.

And then Anna. I hadn't wanted her there for the birth, but she wanted to see the baby, so at the end of it all Anna came into the room.

I couldn't walk because of the epidural. The midwife had promised that I'd be free to leave soon after the birth, she would provide the aftercare, there was no need to remain in hospital, but they wouldn't let me leave until my legs thawed. I was going to have to be wheeled upstairs and remain in a hospital bed until then.

I asked Anna to stay. I was terrified of being alone. I wanted to be home, but I didn't even know where that was. She was the closest thing I had ever known to home. Incapacitated and afraid, I would take whatever remnant or reminder of home that I could get.

It was two in the morning, and I asked Anna to lie down beside me in the hospital bed. We lay rigid, not touching, the baby quiet.

13

Tita, bathed in weak sunlight, was waiting for us on the front porch in flip-flops, leggings and an old T-shirt of mine. Tita, whom I barely knew and who barely knew me.

"You blow, Mum?" she asked.

The baby and I were still covered in blood; her hair caked with it, my cheeks, chest and thighs streaked red.

Yes, I told her, I blew.

She thinks I am strong. The women she worked for in Hong Kong and Singapore all had C-sections. They all had husbands as well. Tita held out her arms toward this long-awaited baby. I still couldn't quite believe there was a baby. She was a sweet, quiet, little egg of a thing, but a near-complete stranger. Who are you? I wanted to ask. I had known her on the inside. Her restless feet and hiccups. Her flips, punches and rolls. But now, outside my body, she was alien to me.

And yet here we were, entering my house that was now our house, my bedroom, now our bedroom, settling into my bed that was now ours. Here she was turning to me every two hours to feed. Feed on what, though? There was no milk. She cried, tried to feed, cried again, gave up, dozed. She woke up two hours later, cried, tried to feed, cried again, dozed. It was excruciating for both of us, nothing natural about it. We were failing in the most fundamental of ways.

Anna held the baby, changed her diaper, swaddled her in pink. She propped a pillow behind my back while I tried to breastfeed. She was practical and efficient, but she couldn't give me what I needed most in that moment. It was brutal to be in her presence at my most open-wounded.

In the precious hours I slept I had nightmares and woke up crying. I fell asleep crying, for that matter. I cried in the time between waking up and falling asleep.

My sense of isolation was acute: we were four strangers in this house, no clear emotional ties between us, not even the connection I should feel to my baby. I had a sense of random bodies on water after a shipwreck, of gulping and gasping for air in the rough dark, of reaching but finding nothing solid to take hold of.

And then it was evening, the day over. Tita retired to her room. Anna left. And I was alone with a newborn. I'd never held a newborn until the night before, never changed one or fed one before that day. I was terrified to be alone with her. I was terrified to be alone. I was supposed to be feeling things that would triumph over terror. I was supposed to be feeling love. But all I felt was an acute sense of alienation. My baby and I were not in this together. Neither of us knew who we were or what we were doing. I felt very afraid for us both.

Later that night, an overwhelming transformation occurred. This dozing, placid baby erupted into a writhing, distressed creature with a big set of lungs. I would eventually discover a whole sheet about this second night in the literature the hospital sent me home with, but who had had time to read it? I would get to the page describing the baby's sudden shock at her change in circumstances about a month too late. For the time being, I was beside myself, weeping from my inability to breastfeed or otherwise console her, agonized by the sight of her tiny, trembling tongue, the pink back of her throat, the rawness of my own battered, stitched and bleeding body doing lunges around the room as I had once seen someone else do with an inconsolable baby.

This went on for hours. I had slept only intermittently over the past five days. I was going to break. I didn't feel there was anyone I could call.

But there *was* another adult in my house. I didn't

know what else to do. I knocked timidly on Tita's door.

She was half-asleep, her long black hair loose around her shoulders. She saw my distress. "It's okay, Mum," she said, grabbing the duvet off her bed. "We do shift work. We be a team."

She laid the duvet down on our bedroom floor in that narrow space between the bed and the closet. It felt like the three of us were aboard a life raft; lone survivors in the middle of a vast ocean, too concerned with simply staying afloat to even scour the horizon for something that looked like land.

Tita, thankfully, knew some basic survival techniques. She picked that baby up and asked her: What's wrong, baby, are you hungry? Are you cold? Your diaper full? Your clothes tight? She talked to that baby until that baby made sense to her. She communicated that sense to me.

14

That first week was like an English winter: all black nights and grey days. Time didn't progress; the same two hours just repeated over and over. The focus was on feeding, getting enough liquid into this baby. A product of my culture and generation, I was determined to breastfeed, but I was expressing only a tiny amount of milk, in so much pain for all the trying, and the little thing was losing more weight than she should.

The midwife visited twice a day, trying to help us get the hang of it. She brought me fenugreek and milk thistle to increase milk supply and a gravity-feed tube to use in the meantime. I pumped what I could into a bottle, pulled it up into the tube, put it into the baby's mouth as if she were a bird. It required four hands, four hands every two to three hours. Tita's hands, my mother's, Anna's.

Only Tita's presence offered some comfort. With the exception of weekends, Tita was always there, discreetly omnipresent, kind. She could hear the baby crying from her room—the walls were paper-thin, just the bathroom separating her room from ours. You could hear everything in this house everywhere in this house— the shower, the sink, the toilet, the dishwasher, the splat of the mail landing in the front hall, Tita's conversations with relatives thousands of miles away, my crying, hers.

It was two o'clock one morning and the baby's cries had once again woken Tita. There she was standing in the doorway. I had trusted that with my baby's arrival instinct would just take over, but there was nothing instinctive about this to me.

It wasn't just the practical help for which I was grateful, but the simple, uncomplicated presence of another person. I had fallen down a deep well, a well full of glue, but Tita was there at the top, leaning over the side, calling out my name.

Then, morning again and there, hazy through the translucence, stood the midwife. I was living my life in the twelve-hour intervals between her visits. But I didn't think she could hear me through the glue. Voices warbled over the top of the well. I reached up, my arm long, my hand grasping. I heard my voice say: I was worth something.

The midwife looked at me like you might look at a person who has lost a leg but thinks it is still there.

It was the best I could do through the glue to communicate my desperation.

The milk still didn't come. After a humiliating hour with a lactation consultant, my midwife sent me to my doctor for a prescription for domperidone, to increase milk supply. My doctor seemed more concerned about my mood than my failure to breastfeed. My midwife had called her expressing concern. It turned out she had not been visiting me twice a day simply because of the breastfeeding issue. This was not the reason the parenting mediator was calling me twice a day either. I cried all the time before the baby was born, but apparently crying all the time *after* a baby is born is a problem. A doctor, a midwife and a therapist were all concerned that I had postpartum depression.

When does grief and fear and exhaustion become depression? I couldn't be depressed, not now. I was afraid of a diagnosis, of its implications.

I said to my doctor, "I'm not thinking about harming myself or my baby, if that's what you're worried about."

"Listen, Camilla, crying all the time? It's not normal."

I remember holding up my hennaed hands, trying to convince three British psychiatrists that I had legitimate reasons for feeling as I did.

My reasons didn't matter. They didn't matter then, they didn't matter in this moment.

I felt this hazy cloud of collusion—voices speaking above me, no one speaking down into the well, no one looking me in the eye—hovering above.

I had been spared any real depression for so many years. I hadn't taken a pill in almost a decade. I was once again disembodied: the woman who had walked into Dr. P's office thirteen years before. I would take the pills the doctor was prescribing. Because this time I was at risk of losing more than my autonomy.

It was the middle of the night again and I was wondering how I was going to survive. I was reminded of another writer asking much the same question in the middle of another night, alone with his infant son. Ian Brown's *The Boy in the Moon*, a memoir of a man seeking sense and connection to a severely disabled child, was the only book I had managed to read all year.

The first months of a baby's life are all hunger, all need. What if you cannot fulfill those needs? What if that need never ends?

"I could feel the heavy tragic years coming on ahead of me, as certain as bad weather," Brown writes; "there were nights when I even welcomed them. At last a fate I didn't have to choose, a destiny I couldn't avoid. There was a tiny prick of light in that thought, the relief of submitting to the unavoidable. Otherwise, they were the worst nights of my life. I can't explain why I wouldn't change them."

I copied those words down into a red notebook. I read them over and over again, trying to suck the life in them into me. *A tiny prick of light.* Neither Ian Brown nor his wife slept uninterrupted for two nights in a row for the first eight years of their son's life. And that heavy certainty of the years ahead. Where did he find that glimmer? When does the weight of circumstances tip into something so leaden that there is not even the tiniest glow in the furthest distance? Where light ceases to even be possible in the imagination.

I found myself emailing Ian, an acquaintance, in the middle of the night. I have no idea what I said. I hope I said thank you; that in a year of only the barest reading, his were the only words that had really reached me.

Just write it all down, he emailed back. Write it all down because you must.

"We tell ourselves stories in order to live," Joan Didion has written. I had an obligation to live; motherhood takes away any other option. And writing is the only way I know how.

A red notebook lay to one side of me every night, a swaddled baby on the other. I believed that if I could find words, I could be a human again. And if I could be a human again, perhaps I could be a mother.

Clench clench these strong teeth in this strong mouth. My mouth. Of my body. This is me speaking, not mouthing, began a draft of a first novel written a lifetime ago. I was scared then, too. Scared to speak, scared to tell a story. But even more scared not to.

15

The only privacy I had was inside my head. Tita lowered me into the bath, cleaned the breast pump, propped me up, changed bloodied sheets, washed them, saw the hours of tears. I apologized, embarrassed. I had no choice. Neither did she. She was unembarrassed, matter-of-fact.

When I had first interviewed her, I had asked her what she wanted from me. Respect was what she said, that was all. She accorded me, at my most undignified, that as well.

I apologized for the messiness of my situation. For the intensity of it all and what it required of her. I asked her how she was finding it so far, living here, whether she felt she was getting the respect she deserved.

Tita sat down on the end of my bed while I fed the baby. She started to tell me something about her experience so far in Canada. The Filipino agency that had brought her to Toronto from Hong Kong two years before had told her she would be working for a "difficult employer," but said they had no doubt she would be up to the task. Tita took care of their children and was expected to oversee their homework, in a second language, one she doesn't speak. She could recognize tone of voice, though. When the parents spoke at the dinner table, they not only excluded her but talked about her. The children picked up on their parents' disregard; during the day they hurled insults, trekked mud quite deliberately across newly washed floors, and spat toothpaste in her face. She didn't blame them, though. She loved them.

She loved the children and cleaned their house, did the laundry, ironing, shopping, cooking, gardening, snow shovelling. And she was yelled at every single day. For leaving a light on, for wasting an egg, for simply being in the line of fire. She was threatened with being deported, told she couldn't use the dishwasher or use the washing machine for her own clothes. She had to buy her own mug from which to drink tea, keeping it in her room. She was not allowed visitors; she was never even given her own key.

They expected her to leave at seven-thirty on Friday night and not return until late Sunday. And go where, exactly? They didn't care. She was forced to trek to the bus stop on cold, dark winter nights where she would wait as long as half an hour on a lonely stretch of unlit road in the suburbs. She bought a winter hat and found refuge with an elderly Filipina lady. But the old lady was of modest means and Tita couldn't use the washing machine at her place either. She took her bedsheets to this woman's apartment in her knapsack, washed them in the bathtub, then hung them over the shower rail to dry.

She sat at the end of my bed while I fed this little baby and cried at the memory of it.

"I didn't think I could survive another year," she said. But she was too afraid of being fired or deported to raise any objection. All nannies in her position are afraid. They are powerless, at the mercy of their employers, to whom their work permits are exclusively tied, and of the exploitative agencies that keep them indentured. It took Tita two years to repay the agency the fee they charged for placing her with employers who, it turned out, had burned through ten nannies in as many years.

When those employers decided to go on holiday for a month, they told her she would not be paid. And so when they left on holiday, Tita left their house for good, rendered homeless and jobless, with a work permit that prevented her from working for anyone else and an entire family back home dependent upon her income. Her former employer still owed her two weeks' pay and a record of employment. That was a fight I was willing to take on. If there was anything I could do for her, it was this.

So we were both, it turned out, reeling from a traumatic year. Neither of us had any reason to trust the other, and yet we were forced into this mutually dependent relationship where trust just had to be.

We did shift work, a baby being passed between us. Whoever had the free hands made dinner—that was our unspoken arrangement. We were, as she had said from the beginning, a team.

16

Twelve days after giving birth, I was on a stage, talking about a book I had written in some other lifetime. I wasn't nervous—not about speaking that morning or about reactions to the book—because I was no longer the woman who wrote that book. The woman who was standing on stage was that woman turned inside out: only the clothes and the tangible evidence of printed pages concealed the truth. I was an empty body asking a limited brain to do all the work.

Perhaps one needs a three-hour break from a baby in the first two weeks in order to fully comprehend what has happened. I couldn't feel anything that morning except my daughter's absence. I was incomplete. I had become a *we*. Was I not *me* without her? Was she *she*? Was this love? I had no idea; it didn't feel like anything I'd ever felt before. I just knew that I had to get home right away. That we had to breathe each other in. Skin on skin. That we must be *we*; our very survival depended upon it.

"She's so good," I say to Anna, who has spent these hours with her. "How did I get such a good baby?"

"Because you deserve it," she replies.

17

For the first time in a long time I was aware of the sun shining. Perhaps the antidepressants had begun to work: edges were becoming discernible; the haze that had dulled everything burning off like a morning fog. The fall leaves were a fire of red and orange, the weather was brisk. We were at Riverdale Farm, a little oasis in the middle of the city, the egg strapped into the BabyBjörn, blinking into the sunlight, her eyes that deep-water navy of all newborns.

Tita was shuffling her feet, unimpressed. "Smells like my country," she said.

She comes from a poor farming community on the Visayan island of Bohol. She grew up on a small farm, the second youngest of four children. Her father had given each of his children a plot of his land on which to build their own houses. Tita was so far the only one who had been able to do so; Tita, the first of two children to go abroad. It had been nine years by this point, first in Singapore, then in Hong Kong, now Toronto. Nine years of minimum-wage labour and she had built her family back home a house.

I had seen the photographs of it posted on her sister's Facebook page. The new house had two bedrooms and indoor plumbing. Tita had just had a white granite floor installed in the living room. Her parents were critical of it, saying it would get filthy. But that way, Tita countered, you can see the dirt. Nine years before, when Tita had told her mother she was going abroad to work as a nanny, her mother had asked her what she was thinking. But you can't even tidy up your room! she had said. Now her parents, younger sister and husband were living in a house with white granite floors while Tita tidied up other people's messes far away.

She missed her husband, Nico, terribly. They spoke on the phone every night. B1 and B2, they called each other: "Babes." They'd been married for four years but had seen each other only twice since the wedding, only once since Tita had arrived in Canada. They were applying for permanent residency as a couple. It would be at least a couple of years before he arrived. In the meantime, he had overseen construction of the new house and was trying his hand at raising pigs.

"What do you think of these pigs?" I asked Tita, leaning on the fence at Riverdale Farm.

"Useless," she said. "Smaller than the pigs in my place."

She told me that at one point during her university education in the island capital, Tagbilaran, her parents could no longer afford the tuition. Tita was already working half-days so she could pay for her board. She was forced to drop out of school. She went to Cebu, a larger island nearby, to get a job. After six months her mother called and said: You can come back—the pig is getting fat. That pig paid her tuition. Two more saw her through to graduation.

"What do you think Nico will do when he gets here?" I asked her.

Tita shrugged. "It doesn't matter," she said. "Factory job."

They would begin to build a new life together. Maybe one day they'd have a child of their own. The sacrifices they have both been willing to make for the prospect of a better future.

Anna and I hadn't had to sacrifice anything. Our commitment was never tested in this way. Our livelihoods did not depend on each other in the ways that exist in a family like Tita's. Our choices had not been limited by poverty, lack of opportunity, citizenship. It is no more than a lucky accident that we were born in the West, that we should find ourselves and each other in a country where the laws would shift during our lifetimes in favour of our rights to marry and raise children.

"If you marry, you must be sure," Tita said. "It is not like food that is too hot and spicy and you can spit out. You have to swallow."

Oh, I swallowed, Tita. Hook, line and sinker. The hook, in fact, is still inside me.

18

At three weeks, my daughter took her first plane ride. We were on a book tour from Montreal, to the east of us, to Vancouver in the west.

I took the baby with me to interviews. She sat in Tita's lap and stared at the lights in radio stations while I was on-air. She stared at walls of books in bookstores. She was part of the story of the person who wrote the book that brought us here. I couldn't compartmentalize my roles as writer and mother; her life was not separate from mine, my life not separate from hers—not even my body was yet.

The day we arrived in Calgary she smiled her first smile. At just six weeks, she was speaking to us from her inner world. Hello, tiny person. How much easier it becomes to speak aloud inanely when there is a someone responding back.

I had last read at the writers' festival in Calgary eight years before. When I arrived at my hotel then, a message had been waiting for me. It said simply: your father called. I felt my stomach burn as I read those words. My father? Was it possible that whoever took the message had misheard? I knew my father was in Calgary thanks to the private detective I had hired a couple of years before, but the chances of his knowing I was in the city seemed remote.

I called the festival director right away. I was afraid, not least because much of the book was about my father. What if he turned up at the reading? What if he made a scene? I didn't even think I could step on stage wondering if he was out there in the audience.

Anne, the director, was wonderful. She and her assistant locked arms with me that night as we moved through the atrium of the theatre. A tall, lean man came toward me. He said: "I am a friend of your father's. He is here."

I felt my knees buckle.

Seeing my reaction, the man added: "He looks good. He bought a new jacket."

Anne and her assistant kept me standing and moved me through the hall.

I have no recollection of getting on stage and doing the reading.

Afterwards I sat at a table between two other writers, Anne's assistant standing guard behind me. A large man was talking to me about a dog he'd once had, a dog named Blue, like one of the characters in my novel. That much I remember. Behind him I suddenly saw a weather-beaten man clutching a book, my book, between his hands. He looked hunted. Haunted. And I started to burn with guilt and anxiety and fear.

The large man moved aside. Now my father was standing right in front of me. He opened his mouth and spoke. I fixated on his teeth, black nubs like charred kernels of corn. He wanted me to sign his book.

I stammered: "I don't know what to write."

"Why don't you write: To Dad, love Moo." It was the pet name he'd given me as a child.

He'd bought a new jacket. And a ticket for the event. And a book. How much had it all cost him? He couldn't afford any of this. Why was he here?

He asked if I would meet him for coffee the next day. Since it could have been so much worse and I was down to monosyllables, I said um, yes.

The next morning we sat in the cafeteria of city hall, where a cup of coffee was only sixty-five cents and smoking was still allowed, as if time had stopped in 1980. He rolled a cigarette between his sepia-stained fingers and threw back mouthfuls of black coffee. He was a man without a filter, telling me things that didn't make a lot of sense, theorizing about incidents in his personal history, trying to link cause and effect.

"The world terrifies me," he confided.

"You mean the people in it."

"Yes."

"But you assume everyone is hostile," I said.

On this, he completely agreed.

"It must be very painful to move in the world," I said, as if Dr. P had replaced me at the table.

It was painful, so he didn't move. He hid, eked out, scammed, squeaked by and drank himself to sleep every night. He described himself as asocial—"Not anti-social," he told me, "but asocial." He called himself "the world's ultimate loner." He said he couldn't have rela-tionships, that he had never actually loved anyone, except his daughter, because she loved him uncondition-ally, at least she had once, when she was small.

I was steely: resolved to be unmoved. I could listen, but I wouldn't absorb it.

He was introspective, or perhaps desperate enough to ask tough questions about why he was the way he was. He wondered if it was because he was dropped on his head as a baby, or because he was put in an orphanage temporarily as a toddler, where he was punished by being tied to a banister. He wondered if it was because he was sent off to boarding school at such a young age, molested by the headmaster, bullied by other boys. He wondered if it was the army.

He told me my first novel had devastated him. Every day he would go to the same bar and nurse two beers before going home to drink a lot more. The waitress there was kind to him—talked to him, let him linger. He told her that he had a daughter who was a writer and that she'd written a book that had gutted him. Perhaps this woman read the book, I can't remember, but what she said in reply helped shift his thinking. "But it's not really about you," she said. "It's about her."

And then, he said, he understood. He understood that the novel was about a secret, a family secret I couldn't talk about. Once, long ago, he told me, he'd been in such a blind rage that he had come home from work and kicked our dog to death.

"I hated myself for doing that," he said. "I abhor violence. It sickens me, it makes me physically ill.

"You must have a memory of it," he said. "You were old enough."

"I don't," I said with conviction.

"You've repressed it, then," he said, insisting that this was what the book was about.

I didn't even know we'd ever had a dog. He could tell himself what the novel was about; he could tell himself whatever he needed to. But he couldn't tell me.

I haven't seen my father since that coffee in 2002. I have wondered whether he was disappointed by my subsequent novels because there was nothing in them that suggested he existed. People are funny that way, I've discovered. Sometimes they would rather be demonized in a story than left out of it.

I would be reading at the same opening night where my father had been in the audience eight years before. I knew somehow that he wouldn't be there this time, but part of me had been hoping he might. I just wanted to tell him one thing: that he had a granddaughter. I wanted to remind him of something he had once felt: of being loved unconditionally, as he had been by his daughter, when she was small.

19

I introduced my daughter to Ara instead. We had become reacquainted ten years before, when I sent him a copy of my first novel. In that novel, a single mother meets a younger man—a Sikh at medical school—a gentle and imaginative man from another world. His presence transforms both the mother and her daughter. A brooding, damaged girl blossoms in the short time Suresh lives with them; a mother's mood grows light.

Ara had written back to me, shocked and flattered. He didn't understand how he could have been a source of inspiration. What might have seemed a short time in his own life had echoed for years in mine.

After moving out West, Ara had changed his first

name to Alan, chopped the Armenian suffix off his surname, given up acting and become a chartered accountant. I had been disappointed that he had discarded so much of what I had romanticized over the years, but I needn't have been. When we met a couple of years later it was immediately obvious that although he had taken on a public persona that was anglicized, respectable and conventional, he remained himself—Ara the slightly mad Armenian, volcanic with expression.

We meet whenever I'm in Vancouver. He calls me his daughter; he never did have children of his own.

Tita and I were waiting for him in a restaurant overlooking the water. It had been a beautiful warm fall day, and now night, everything sparkled—the water, the boats, the candles on the tables.

Alan was still Ara. He walked into the restaurant, filling all the space around him, and embraced me with the biggest of bear hugs. He shook Tita's hand in both of his, then fearlessly picked up the egg. He held her high, astonished. He rocked her little being back and forth and made the funny faces he had made for my brother and me as children. She responded—she had a voice now, a soft, husky voice in addition to her smile.

We sat close together on one side of a round table. Ara-Alan said: "I have to come to Toronto. I should move to Toronto!" He had not been back to Toronto since he left us thirty years ago, I reminded him, not a single visit in all those years. "But I have a granddaughter now," he said.

We talked about my mother, my brother, his mother, his wife. We talked about my life and his. We talked about the past, but more about the present. We talked about this remarkable creature in my arms.

Then Tita, whom I had taken to calling the resident psychologist, said to Ara: "Why did you and Camilla's mother break up?"

An excellent question. Why hadn't it ever occurred to me to ask it? He had left so abruptly. So had David, for that matter. And my father. And Anna.

My best conclusion is that people do what they need to do for themselves and ultimately that trumps any other consideration. Perhaps they want to spare you by not telling you much. Perhaps they just want to spare themselves. Without the whole story, though, you are left with only shards of evidence and your own imagination, bits out of which to construct a story that might allow you, eventually, in a best-case scenario, to integrate the loss and continue living. Or else you just continue to spin: to speculate and obsess, much as I had been doing for the past ten months.

Tita had opened up the space for the possibility of an answer that could perhaps give me some understanding of a recurrent theme in my life.

"Ah," said Ara, "that is something we agreed to never tell the children."

"But I'm not a child anymore," I said.

At just that moment, another writer passed by, brushed my shoulder, said hi. I looked up and realized the restaurant had filled with fellow writers, most of whom I have met over the years. Many of them were there with their spouses. I am usually on my own at writers' festivals. I tend to feel shy and awkward in these situations, so I most often disappear into my room rather than linger in public spaces. I don't eat alone in public or visit the hospitality suite to socialize. I treat these trips as work.

I had more enthusiasm for these things at the beginning of my career. But then once, in fact not that long ago, I found myself very far away in the company of writers from around the world who seemed a good deal more important. One of them told me I was beautiful—from the nose down. The rest—my eyes, my forehead—she said, waving her hands around her ears, looked like that of a crazy person.

I have no idea who she was. She was just a stranger who stripped me of any strength, peeling away my thin exterior to expose what I felt was some inescapable truth. We were in Bali, a place of improbable beauty, and all I wanted was to be home, with Anna, that rare person who could give me back my skin.

"I'm not a child anymore," I repeated once the writer I knew had gone back to his table.

"I made an agreement with your mother," Ara said, shaking his head.

The writer was now beckoning to me from his table. I excused myself, picked up my daughter and went to introduce her to the other writers seated there. I didn't feel the slightest bit awkward or shy. I agreed to meet them in the hospitality suite later. It was as if having a child had suddenly allowed me to assume my place as a member of the species.

Later that night I would call my mother. I would ask her what she and Ara had agreed not to tell the children.

I have no idea what he's talking about, she would say, leaving me, once again, to my imagination.

20

The company Anna worked for had an office in Vancouver, so she timed a business trip around our being there. She came and took the baby for walks while I caught up on sleep. She hung out with the baby in our hotel room while I did my readings onstage. She held the baby on the flight we shared home. I saw the woman I loved. The family I had imagined.

The morning after we returned to Toronto, I left the egg with Tita to go grocery shopping. I was loading up a cart with diapers, formula, fruit and vegetables for an empty fridge when I heard the ping of an incoming text. It was from Anna. No biggie, she prefaced her news. She wanted to give me the heads-up that she'd recently had a date with a woman who was a friend of both of ours. The same friend who had invited us to her daughter's hockey practice. The night I was too exhausted to go. The night Anna ended our marriage.

My knees started to shake. Anna is not a dater. She is a decision maker. This was, in fact, one of the things I loved about her. Ten years before, I had been the decision.

So here it was: the fatal blow.

Anna was not coming home. She had never been coming home.

My stomach felt as if it was full of razor blades. I am not the first woman to have felt this, nor the last. The particulars of my circumstances were a bit unusual, but the situation was not. You have a baby at home, an empty fridge, groceries to deliver. It doesn't matter that you are bleeding all over the grocery store floor. You have to stand. You have to stand. The fuck. Up.

21

Words begin to spill out in the middle of the night: fragments, short staccato sentences—the rhythm of pain and fury. I take up my neglected pen. The first thing I write is that I must write because I want to scream and pound my head against a wall but I cannot scream and pound my head against a wall because I have a baby. Because the person I wish could hear my rage isn't listening and the person who shouldn't hear any of it is right here, breathing bubbles, dreaming of milky boobs and first snow.

The love I feel for my child, the love that feels like ache in the marrow, does not mitigate or murder the anger. They exist together, a potent soup in the stomach.

I would take a knife to myself to stop the feeling if I could. But I am trapped.

It is the end all over again, and perhaps worse: the death of the remaining fantasies, the delusions of reunion that have sustained me over the course of the past few months. Anna is not coming home. She has never been coming home. I'm looking upon the scene of a murder and all I have is my notebook and pen.

part three

roost

I

I am standing in the doorway of our bedroom, hovering like a ghost in a frame. I watch Tita with her wide eyes and big smile, leaping like a frog for my daughter's amusement. I just don't have it in me, I think, standing at a remove, that capacity for joy or abandon.

It should be my daughter's other parent playing peek-a-boo in this moment, me watching her lose all inhibition—becoming innocent and childlike—and welling up with love for them both. It should be my partner seeing me anew, at greater depth, as a mother, moved by the brave extent of what we are capable of as humans, amazed by how far we can travel in the course of a lifetime, to this place of love that is so stripped bare, so elemental.

Is it possible to mourn what should have been? What never even was? Not even those first weeks of this pregnancy were happy. If I look back on it now, Anna was already gone. At the time, I just trusted in the bigger commitment we had made to each other. But perhaps I was just unwilling to face the possibility that I might be doing this on my own. That Anna might want something, or someone, else.

Our blind spots are of our own making. They protect our sense not of how things are but of how we wish or need them to be.

I stand here watching Tita leaping like a frog and wonder where she finds it. She, who is burdened with so much, the lives of at least ten other people on an island far away, still possesses the capacity to be light, to be free. How lucky my daughter is that someone in the house can make her laugh like this. How grateful I am. But Tita won't be here forever. Without Tita, I fear my daughter will know the extent of my sadness.

Tita still misses the children she looked after in Hong Kong and Singapore. She loved them; they loved her. She has been the primary support to five mothers now, four of them with husbands. Most painful of all, she remains separated from the man with whom she hopes to have children.

It is not uncomplicated for either of us.

2

Tita leaves on Friday nights to spend the weekend with her elderly Filipina friend. I dread the long and lonely weekend, the boredom, the hours, the exhaustion, the early mornings. The weekends are for families. My friends are with their own.

I take the egg to 24-hour grocery stores and drug-stores, spend hours wandering the aisles. I take her to empty parks twice a day, push her through winter winds in her stroller, drink more coffee than I feel like drinking, drive without destination trying to get her to sleep.

I knock on my neighbour's door when I feel desperate in the early morning, drop in for a visit, finding her and her husband and kids having breakfast in their pyjamas.

I have no pride anymore; I am well beyond the possibility of humiliation.

I invite myself over to Heidi's house in the afternoons and stay on for dinner with her and her boyfriend. I lay the egg down to sleep in their spare bedroom and crawl into bed beside her later. I feed her and bundle her up when she wakes, feeling guilty for taking up this kind of room in Heidi's house, for my inability to settle into being alone at home with my daughter.

I cry too much when it's just the two of us. I cry and count the hours. The only joy I am able to take in my daughter is seeing her through the eyes of others. Being outside my experience offers a glimpse of what might have otherwise been.

I leave Heidi's house and take my baby out into the cold, dark middle-of-the-night. I go to the downtrodden mall near my house before any of the stores are open. I sit on a bench, my baby in her stroller, and burst into tears. I call the parenting mediator as soon as dawn breaks.

Get out of that ugly mall, she says. Go somewhere beautiful.

But you don't understand, I say. There is nowhere beautiful.

You need people, she says. You need new friends.

A lot of friends fall away when you have a baby; a natural evolution. You just can't do the things you used to do. You don't have the time, the energy, the attention, perhaps the inclination. You might try to participate for the first little while, as I did, afraid of disappearing, only to realize the extent to which your rhythm and focus have changed.

The life I used to know carries on without me.

I have some idealized notion that the loss of friends and the lifestyle you used to share is eased when you are part of a couple. You have each other to share in the wonder and exhaustion of it all. You're different, but different together. You have sidestepped out of the world you used to know, but there is love in the new place, and so you are warm and surrounded. I have married friends with children who have tried to disabuse me of any such romance, but still, the fantasy persists.

You lose friends, too, for so many different reasons, when you are no longer part of a couple. Not immediately, necessarily, but over time. You try to hold on to people for different reasons, but the tacit knowledge they have about your former spouse, their ongoing friendships with her, and the embrace of her new girlfriend who was also once your friend, make it painful and impossible.

You lose friends in grief. Grief turns you into a foreigner in a world you used to know; its persistence can render you a depressed and undesirable alien. People prefer you at a distance where there is less danger of contagion. If you have to appear in public, you must at least have the courtesy to wear a mask.

3

One change I did not anticipate is how much more present my mother and stepfather would be in my life. I have produced their only grandchild. My mother's feelings toward her granddaughter have an intensity I have never seen in her.

My mother's parents are dead, her brother far away, her first husband, my father, long gone. Her son is back, though for how long we're not certain. But she and I are no longer just the two survivors of a family; we are, with my daughter, now a line. I wonder if my mother looks at us and thinks: I created this. Two generations. Two full and complicated beings.

I think about those who came before—her parents,

my grandparents. They were cold as a frozen lake; rigid, without evidence of fault lines or spring melt. They had denied all existence of interior lives, expressing disdain for anything but the most socially sanctioned, class-determined performance. My grandfather died just a month before my daughter was conceived. He was almost ninety-seven. I had had a lifetime of exposure to him—I'd even spent weeks looking after him in his early nineties when his wife broke her hip—but I never knew anything of his heart or soul. My grandmother, an austere and remote woman, had died when I was a teenager, and I remember my surprise when this news didn't make my mother cry.

But I never loved her, she'd said.

I remember being struck by the fact that not loving a parent was even an option. But of course now I can see that you cannot love someone you do not know, and you cannot feel loved by someone who does not know you. My mother's parents were completely unknowable. She was raised to be unknowable herself; she was raised to be alone, a legacy passed on to my brother and me.

My mother's glow in my daughter's presence can help me momentarily overcome what ails me. It is a gift to be unexpectedly altered in this way, late in life.

My stepfather shares the depth of feeling toward his granddaughter. He did not have children, and my brother and I were too old to become his. When the egg was tiny, either crying or inert, my stepfather kept his distance, afraid to break her. But in just a matter of weeks, now able to smile and coo in response to people, and very responsive to him, she has become his little girl.

I am watching them with their granddaughter. She brings out different sides of each of them, surprises. They are Lola and Lolo, having embraced the Tagalog terms for grandparents offered by Tita, she who has named us all. They are growing into their new roles together, and their love for each other grows bigger as a consequence.

I don't spoil this by talking about my feelings, the persistent pain, the bouts of rage. Yet I can feel my mother simmering with a quiet yet fierce protectiveness toward me.

There has always been a certain wildness about me that I sense she has regarded with some fear. Perhaps it's the aspects of my father that she sees in me and certainly in my brother: the range of moods, a certain defiance of authority, lack of convention, the propensity for darkness. I wonder if I am just as alien and threatening to her as my father was in some ways.

Perhaps I have become more recognizable to her as a mother. Or rather, as a woman on my own with a child. She was alone at my age with two children, her marriage over. I have gained more of a mother from having a baby in these circumstances. But the parenting mediator is right: I do need new friends.

An old friend of mine offers to set me up with someone. I'm in no shape to date—in truth, I won't be for years—but of course there is the fantasy that someone will swoop in and overwhelm the pain, so I agree to meet Harry's friend.

I am a disaster. Melissa is funny as hell and a bit of a disaster herself. There is no way we should be dating, but we like each other too much not to become friends. It's an odd time for a new friendship, particularly with someone who doesn't have children, an odd time when you are breastfeeding and exhausted and crying all the time.

But Melissa is in need of new friends herself. She is from the East Coast, doing her PhD in a neighbouring town, and she misses her home and her family and the Maritime way of life. She is a decade younger than me— the age I was when I met Anna—and lives the itinerant life of a student, a life I used to know, one that has room for the possibility of new friendships. And she has big feelings: both dark and light. We are familiar to each other in these ways. She encounters me in my new life and reminds me that I am someone worth knowing.

Tita calls Melissa Miles, because the town where she lives and goes to school is miles and miles away and because, in Filipino culture, as I am quickly realizing, nicknames are de rigueur.

At the dinner table one night, Tita asks Miles about her thesis. Simply put, she is writing about loneliness and queerness. The intersection of two societal evils.

"So," Tita concludes, a little bewildered. "You are a lonely gay, Miles?"

"Well, Tita," says Miles, laughing, "yes, I guess I am."

I had made so many assumptions about Tita's conservatism in the beginning based on her attendance at church on Sundays and her prayer before every meal and the fact that she apologizes to Jesus every time she throws any leftover food into the organic waste bin; based on footage of self-flagellation in Manila at Easter, and the little I know about Filipino culture, having visited the Philippines on a book tour a few years ago.

We've come a long way since. Tita has introduced me to the fairly elaborate taxonomy of gender and orientation that exists in the Philippines. If I am wearing my boyfriend jeans and boots she will remark that I look *badoy*, which seems to mean butch without being lesbian. Lesbians are all tomboys, regardless of how butch or femme they may be. There are the *double cara*—those who can be either masculine or feminine. Tita's own best friend "used to be tomboy" but is now preparing for her wedding to a man.

Tita thinks of orientation as a fluid proposition. She jokes that her own husband is *bakala*—a gay man—every time he gets the slightest bit sentimental. In Tita's mind, it is actions, rather than proclamations of identity, that make one queer.

Miles fits into that understanding; she left a husband behind in the Maritimes. A man with whom she'd raised a teenager, not as a stepmother as such, more a big sister. She left her island because there was no way to do a PhD in her field there, but also, more importantly, because there was no room there to be gay. She has a heart full of guilt as a consequence. A heart full of guilt and hope and goodness and complicated longing.

As our friendship evolves, she begins to spend the night on the couch after she comes for dinner, which she does at least once a week, because she lives so far away. Increasingly these sleepovers extend into part of the next day. My sense is that she'd rather not go back at all: she hates that town miles and miles away and she loves it here, both being in the city and being here with us. She jokes that she is in the family way. In my house, ours is the simple routine of life with a baby.

Miles designates herself the egg's playmate. She writes stand-up comedy in her free time and tries out her ribald sketches on my daughter. She is boisterous and physical and can make the baby girl laugh in that way Tita can make her laugh. She is long and lean and strong and lifts the egg high in the air for a different view of things. She alters all of our perspectives, in fact. Miles falls easily into our domestic rhythm.

Eat/sleep/play, eat/sleep/play.

4

There will be five of us tonight at the table in my white Ikea kitchen with the bright blue linoleum floor. Through the glass, the leaves are fluttering to the ground. It's cold and blustery outside and I am in the mood to roast a chicken.

Everyone has an opinion on how to roast a chicken. I like to insert half an onion, half a lemon and a few buds of smashed garlic into the cavity, grind liberal amounts of salt and pepper over the skin, slip in slices of garlic here and there, place sprigs of tarragon, if I have them, between the legs and breasts. A few dollops of butter will crisp the skin. And if you're feeling really indulgent, there's always bacon.

My brother, Micah, says: Do it, go for the bacon. He has shot and cooked any number of birds himself. It's the legacy of our English father—what men of a certain class do. I know the taste of lead. I wouldn't know the taste of pheasant or rabbit without it.

That my brother is here in my kitchen expressing an opinion about chicken, that my brother is here in this most ordinary of settings, still strikes me as nothing short of a miracle. He was here at the end of the summer and has now returned to renovate my basement. Tito Mike, Tita calls him.

He is terrified to pick up his niece, though, so afraid that he'll hurt her in some way. I put the baby in his arms a few times just to prove to him that he won't break her. He stands in the kitchen with his shaved head and goatee and his tall frame, every inch of his skin covered in angry ink, and looks amazed and terrified by this little white egg in his arms. He jumps back whenever she sneezes. He pulls up Herb Alpert on my iPod. The egg flails her legs enthusiastically to "Spanish Flea" and "Tijuana Taxi," which never fails to make us laugh.

We take her with us to Home Depot when we go to get building materials. "You know people think you're the father," I say.

"Cool," he says.

Tita and Micah have, I think, a sweet little flirtation going on, though neither of them would ever admit it. They are both beautiful to look at: Tita with her long, thick hair and brown wide-eyed face; Tito Mike tall, dark and handsome beyond the tattoos. He's a man to admire, one with an amazing breadth of talent. He is a visual artist and a silversmith. He earns a living as a welder. He once built his own cabin in the woods.

When Tita tells Micah the story of her last employers and how they still, despite my emails and phone calls to them, owe her two weeks' pay, he gets furious. They claim they cannot pay her until she comes to pick up her things. Tita thinks she might have left a pair of jeans at their house—she can't think of anything else.

My brother offers to accompany her, but as tempting as it is to imagine Tita turning up on a suburban doorstep with a six-foot-two, two-hundred-and-forty-pound tattooed white guy, we realize this may be perceived as threatening. I will carry on with the emails and phone calls. I will be a mosquito buzzing around their heads until they can't stand it anymore.

Micah and Tita are back to talking about food—a shared passion. He worked in a kitchen for years; she learned to cook in Singapore from an old Chinese woman. "I didn't even know how to chop vegetable before," she says. Her father, who was once a cook in a Chinese restaurant on the island of Mindanao, did all the cooking at home when she was growing up. She makes many of her Chinese lola's recipes now.

My tastes were a surprise to her: "You know how to eat spicy?" A meal isn't a meal without a bit of heat, we agree. Tita is at home in our neighbourhood among the Chinese groceries, the Vietnamese restaurants and bakeries. A familiar palate, the taste of home—it matters more than one might realize.

Tita had worked only in the suburbs before coming to live with me, miles of houses, nowhere to go, no spice. She arrived at my house with recipes for quiche. Canadian food, if there is such a definable thing, is boring to her. The one exception is cheese. "You make me so expensive!" Tita says after she tastes aged cheddar for the first time. She and Tito Mike are locusts for aged cheddar. A brick of it will last only three days in our house. When she and Micah win four dollars each on a lottery scratch card, they buy cheese for the house with the winnings.

Last to arrive for dinner tonight is Miles, who is coming in by bus from the grey town miles away. I don't wait to ask her opinion on how to roast a chicken; she has never roasted anything in her life. She cooks Island food—lobster, potatoes, mussels, things boiled in a single pot. On her lonely far-flung island province, "boiled dinner" is a specialty, salt the extent of seasoning.

My kitchen is full of laughter tonight and the egg is strapped to my front in the BabyBjörn. She likes to see everything that's going on; she is at her most content strapped against me, watching my hands work. She is helping me mash potatoes. A little horseradish goes into the pot. Next, she is helping me massage olive oil, lemon and garlic into Swiss chard. She is at the heart of this unlikely circle who will gather around the table for dinner. The grieving single mother, the recovering addict, the lonely gay, the temporary worker and the arthritic cat.

5

And then there are Tuesday evenings. Anna comes to spend time with the egg. I was supposed to marvel in this, witnessing Anna being a parent, but there is no celebration here. And so I leave my house.

On those evenings I usually take myself out for a bowl of *pho* around the corner. I eat soup and read a book. Or I take myself to a movie at the indie theatre down the street. I started going to movies alone when I was pregnant because I was lonely and in need of distraction. I no longer give a fuck that strangers might see it as sad. It's taken half of my adult life and a healthy dose of personal tragedy to finally make me stop feeling the self-consciousness of an adolescent.

On Tuesday evenings I watch documentaries about cave paintings in France and child labour in salt mines in India. I can't tell you much about any of the films I have seen. I can tell you the theatre is under-heated, that it's winter and that my feet are damp and cold. I watch whatever is showing between six and eight, usually missing the end so I can be home the moment Anna leaves. I go to Starbucks if there is still time to kill. I talk to no one and no one talks to me. My face betrays me; it's not a face, but a Tuesday heart.

6

Tita gives me a blow-dryer for Christmas. I don't think she thinks I'm enough of a girl. "For when you go on dates," she says.

Hard to imagine that. I have never been more exhausted in my life. I don't have to want to meet strangers for lunch or coffee or a glass of wine or dinner. I want to be reading the paper or doing the crossword with someone, as I used to do with Anna. She was sports, I was geography. I want to be in my pyjamas and parenting with someone together. I want to be a family. I want to be years into a relationship, in that place where you are known and knowing and loving and loved—the place I thought I was.

"How is your feelings, Mum?" Tita, resident psychologist, asks this morning, as she does from time to time.

I don't always answer the question. I don't always have to.

"You are not a loser, Mum," she says.

I burst into tears. Tita has a way, with her big heart and broken English, of nailing things, and to hear it put so simply cuts me right to the core.

"You are *manhid*," she says, "not ready to love again because your heart is not yet recover." Tita bursts into tears herself then. Tita, who wishes a new relationship for me, who gives me a blow-dryer in the hopes that I might find one, she who has not seen her own husband in two years.

7

Tito Mike is a big male presence, both physically and emotionally. His moods are up and then way down. It's not difficult to gauge where on the spectrum he is; it doesn't demand the kind of vigilance living with an erratic alcoholic does. He's keen to show me the day's work, the nuances of what he has accomplished, but sometimes I'm just a girl who knows nothing about renovations asking stupid questions. He does his best to be patient with me, he treats Tita with the utmost respect, tiptoes around the baby, but he is a man with demons inside.

He spends the nights on the couch in my office because the room he rents is in a small town too far away and he has little money to spend on things like gas. He falls asleep on the couch in his jeans, studded belt and Timberlands. He drinks beer all day long and is both never obviously drunk and perpetually drunk. He wakes up in the middle of the night to go outside to smoke. He yells in his sleep, occasionally sleepwalks, once walking straight into Tita's room, thinking it was his bedroom in the house where we grew up, which had exactly the same layout.

Every few days he complains of nausea and fatigue. He sleeps for half a day, then drags himself up, excusing himself, disappearing back to his rented room, promising to come back and finish the basement as soon as he feels better.

He doesn't take care of himself. The chain-smoking and constant drinking can't be good for him, and he eats erratically and cheaply, eating well only when I am feeding him or he is cooking himself some stolen meat bought from a guy with a duffel bag outside the grocery store nearby. My freezer is full of steak—trunk meat, he calls it: Four bucks! Still frozen!—that I won't touch.

I grow impatient with him—both for the lack of care he shows himself and for the slow progress on the basement—but I recognize how far he has come to get clean, and he is doing me such a huge favour, doing his best, and his best is beautiful, and it's good to have a brother again, even one who fades in and out.

When he returns after three or four days away he is always raring to go, full of life, at the other extreme of his emotional spectrum. I wonder if he might be bipolar. He's good company when he's up. We take the baby out in the stroller, trudging through the snow, and have breakfast at his favourite diner. She sits on Tito Mike's lap while we eat. He calls her babycakes. "My niece," he tells the cook. "Cool, eh?"

For all the complicated feelings my brother has toward our father, Micah still needs to eat bacon and eggs every day just like he used to. Before my father moved to the farm, he used to come and pick us up some Saturday mornings and take us to his favourite diner. We sat in a red booth and he would order himself bacon and eggs and call the waitress "love" or "darling," mortifying us with his misplaced terms of endearment and his accent. My father never asked us if we wanted anything to eat—being both poor and cheap, he conveniently assumed my mother had fed us breakfast—but he would order us vanilla milkshakes that we could see being made in an old-school blender behind the counter. And he gave us quarters for the jukebox.

I had forgotten about the jukebox. These are the kinds of details Micah and I fill in for each other. The ones the other forgets or never knew.

After breakfast we head to Home Depot or make the trek to Ikea, and then Micah gets to work again on the basement, never before noon, breaking for dinner with Tita, the egg, me and often Miles. After dinner he insists on treating us to dessert—Oh Henry! bars, 3 Musketeers, chocolate bars he loved as a kid—and lottery tickets that he buys from the corner store. He calls me Min, Minna. My dad did too. My little brother. Breaks my heart.

8

Tita, the egg and I are taking a respite from winter, visiting friends who are building a house by a Mexican lake. We have left Micah and Miles behind. They're mudding and sanding the basement walls, rebuilding the basement stairs, getting carpet quotes, dealing with the electrician, looking after Leo the cat. Miles should be writing her thesis, but in the spirit of determined procrastination, she has decided instead to learn how to frame a ceiling and install drywall. She's sleeping on the living-room couch in her clothes while Micah sleeps on the couch in my office in his. She says learning how to drywall might come in handy in the future. There are so few academic jobs to be had, especially in the study of lonely gays.

Tita and I walk through the cobblestoned streets of a pretty lakeside town in the late afternoon, taking turns carrying the baby. We stop to buy coconuts. Tita is selective. She knows how to scramble up the trees on her family's land and hack the perfect coconut from its mooring, letting it fall twenty feet to the ground. We perch on a stone wall and drink the juice. The egg reaches for the straw, has her first taste of something other than milk.

We wonder aloud if there is much snow at home and how Miles and Micah are getting on in the basement.

"Wouldn't it be good if they are together, Mum?" Tita says.

"Never going to happen, Tita."

"Why not?"

"Well, for starters, Miles likes girls."

Tita is not convinced. And who am I to argue. What do I honestly know about love and attraction anymore?

The day is ending and the village is coming to life after the long siesta of the afternoon. Shutters unfurl, revealing small grocery stores selling vegetables and tostadas and beer. Taco stands appear on the streets, music plays. Women sit on the front stoops of their small houses and chat with each other, televisions blaring in the background, their children playing in the road.

They would pay us no attention if it weren't for the baby. *Qué linda, preciosa, guapísima*. The baby is the interface between me and the world, and this is heightened in a situation where we do not share a language. The focus has shifted, as I always knew it would. It is evident in the only Spanish I learn: terms of endearment, words for babies.

We stop at a small grocery store to buy lettuce, avocados, tomatoes and green onions for a salad. We can hear singing from the church in the square. The doors are splayed open, congregants still filing in. We follow them and stand at the back of the church. I have done this one other time this year—for Tita, on Christmas Day. My brother had even come with us. We were raised without religion, told we were atheists, that religion provided answers for the weak among us, those who could not tolerate the lack of answers to life's imponderables. This was my father's church. I have no concept of God. But I do have a significant degree of spiritual envy.

Occasionally, Tita will position the egg's hands in prayer and, despite being entirely irreligious, I leave it be. Tita has her own relationship to my daughter. She has ways of interacting with her that are specific to her personality and culture, ways of childrearing that she has learned over her years working as a nanny, and a soft but firm hand.

The first time I thanked Tita for being so affectionate with my daughter, she said: "But how could I be nanny without love?"

That love should be a given. What other job has in its description an implicit expectation of love?

I share with Tita the work, the joys and the memories. And like all intimate relationships, Tita and I have created a shared language: ours is part Tagalog, part Visayan, part baby, part English, part spoken, part not. Ours is a complex interdependence: financial, practical, emotional. Friendship can be hard to negotiate when one person is the boss. Friendship can erode privacy and result in feelings of obligation. I try to be aware of this, but Tita has the added burden of having to intuit and draw boundaries of her own because I am not terribly good at it. The built-in boundaries that would normally exist do not in our case. There is no spouse coming home in the evening to join me in being a parent. There is no one else with whom either of us can share the day.

I miss Tita when she's not with us on the weekends. Not just her help but her company. I like her insights into people, her sense of humour, her imagination and ability to play. I like who she is with my daughter, who my daughter is with her. I like who she is with me. Who I am with her. At home, she disappears when she needs to. She is present where she assumes I need her present. She pulls up the slack when she sees me flagging. I relieve her when I sense she's had enough.

Now we're together, not on a book tour but on holiday. When our friends offer us two separate king-sized beds in rooms at opposite ends of the house, it is Tita who asks if we might share a room. We have shared a room before, in the earliest days with a newborn, but not a bed. It's peaceful; the baby asleep between us.

A friend recently remarked on the peacefulness of

my house, the absence of tension. "It's because I'm a single parent," I said. There's no resentment over who gets to go back to work, keep a career going, engage with other adults, read the newspaper, over who has more time for a social life or exercise, over not having time together as a couple, over not having sex, over whose turn it is to get up in the middle of the night.

But wait: I also have a nanny. And not just any nanny, but Tita. She's three steps ahead in anticipating what both my daughter and I might need. She is so far ahead, in fact, that as Vibika has observed, I never *have* to ask for anything. But I do ask her for advice, for guidance. I appeal to her confidence and expertise with children. She will tell me if she thinks there is a better way. And I will listen. We have a rapport that is so familiar to me it is familial. Tita could well have grown up in an English family. She makes me laugh at times when I find it hardest to. She makes me laugh, most often, at myself.

The church service is well under way and Tita is dabbing her eyes with one of the egg's burping cloths. She kneels on the floor to pray. While Tita is on her knees, praying to God, thinking of home, the egg reaches for the hands of the child of the woman beside me in her mother's arms, trying to stuff them into her mouth. The brown-eyed girl, perhaps two years old, is intrigued, and they play with each other's hands throughout the mass. It feels clichéd to be a romantic about it, but much as Tita is moved by something universal, so am I. Children are children everywhere, curious and uninhibited, encountering the world for the first time with eyes, hands, mouths.

How do you protect a child from heartbreak? All I know is that the egg wants to be held all the time, and perhaps if I hold her all the time she will know that she is loved in such a fundamental and profound way that when her heart is broken as an adult, she will not fall apart, will know she is still loved and lovable.

Micah recently asked if I didn't think she'd grow up spoiled as a result of being carried all the time. He does not think we were spoiled in this way. Perhaps English children of our generation weren't, perhaps my mother just had her hands too full with two of us and a trouble-some husband. I honestly can't remember. Micah's memories start much earlier than mine. I remember best the years when there was no one to change a washer, and I was of no help.

I will ruin the egg in some way, I told Micah, it's in the job description. Given the options, I think this one is pretty good.

9

Micah and Miles have cooked a roast beef to welcome us home. There is a package on the table for Tita. Her last employers have finally sent a cheque and her things after I threatened to contact our MP and a lawyer. Inside the package is a used bar of soap, some men's deodorant, a bath plug and a chipped mug. They have deducted thirty-two dollars—the cost of sending these things by courier—from the amount owed to her. Unbelievable.

Dinner is a prelude to showing us the basement, now complete. Micah and Miles are bursting with pride and accomplishment, having done a beautiful job. They have made me a proper office with a desk and bookshelves and a closet. I can move out of the bedroom I've been sharing with my daughter and into the bedroom that has served as a neglected office until now. I can sleep on my own and work in the basement. I can try to write again.

That's the idea, in any case. Instead, I find myself buying my brother a bed, duvet, sheets, pillows, towels and two sets of pyjamas, and Micah moves into the space he has just finished renovating. He will live in the basement, giving up the room he rents and rarely uses in a town an hour and a half away.

Now that he lives with us full-time, the pattern of his moods is clear. I irritate him with questions, trying to diagnose him, wanting to help him find relief.

He finally admits that he is trying to wean himself off methadone. I hadn't understood that being clean can mean that while you are free of a particular drug, you are hooked on something else in its place. Something legal, prescribed and, arguably, even more addictive than the drug you have just quit, sold as a "cure."

He doesn't think methadone is any kind of solution—liquid handcuffs, he calls it—but the clinic will not reduce his dose. And so he has chosen to withdraw from it himself. He describes this as the feeling of his bones being crushed, ants crawling over the pulverized ruins, his guts liquid. He takes the edge off with other opiates, prescription pills bought or begged off the street, as most people trying to get off methadone do, but he's developed a high tolerance for those; he takes enough of them every day to kill a person, and they no longer even blunt the edge. When he can't take it anymore, he hauls himself to the nearest methadone clinic. Unfortunately, the longer he waits between visits to the clinic, the more room his dark moods occupy.

I'm angry at his failure to disclose this while at the same time feeling immensely proud of him. I still want him here. He's safer here than anywhere. A grown man is trying to liberate himself from drugs in the presence of a baby. She is pure and innocent and uncontaminated. He becomes a baby himself, down to basic bodily functions. He is trying to rewind the decades, start again.

And I'm the mother. He emerges from the basement after three or four days of sleep, not having eaten that whole time. I make him something manly to eat, then present him with a list of chores. I keep him busy, focused. He behaves well because he doesn't want to lose me again and because he feels ashamed and because there is a baby in our midst. He knows that the baby comes before everyone. He is exceptionally well mannered, deferential to us all. I love him more than I have ever loved him in my life.

10

Tito Mike feeds the baby her first solid food at five months. Tita, Miles and I watch in anticipation. This is a *major* event. We are poised to video the moment for Lola and Lolo.

"Let her play with it first," I direct Micah. "Let her smell it, touch it, paint her highchair with it if she wants to." I'm repeating something I read in a book.

The egg just opens her mouth and swallows the mashed avocado off the spoon Tito Mike is holding as if she does it every day.

"She's eating!" he shouts, far more astonished than she is. He's as proud of himself as he is of her.

He's proud of me, too; he keeps telling me so. He would like nothing more than to have a baby and a house.

He's talking about moving to Vancouver. He needs a new life and he doesn't feel, given his past associations, that he can reinvent himself here. My brother hopes not to be alone in his new life. There's a mess of a girl who pecks holes in his heart; he hopes she will join him in Vancouver. After she's finished her sentence.

He'll build a white picket fence around them and they'll get a dog and have a baby. A union job might be the way to go, he tells me: overtime, benefits, workers' comp.

We need some air in this house. It's been a long and intense winter with too many big personalities in too small a space, but I don't want him moving so far away and I don't like the sound of this girl one bit.

"Can't you at least stay in the city?" I ask him. He is making new associations here, after all, with us. He's Tito Mike. I want my daughter to have an uncle. I'm afraid to lose him again. Afraid to lose this family, however fragile, that we have formed.

If I can keep my brother in projects, perhaps I can hold on to him long enough that he will discover he has reinvented himself here with us. My backyard, for instance. The snow melts and spring reveals the extent of the disaster. A leaning fence pushed out by the stubborn roots of Manitoba maples frames a square of red brick and flagstone, both ugly and problematic—water puddles on the surface, taking days to seep away. It is likely seeping right into my basement—by the end of March we've had two floods.

I did a lot of staring at this backyard last summer, watching the light through the trees, imagining what this hard surface could otherwise be. A lot of staring and not much else.

I like the containment of a garden. I like the possibilities, the constant shifting within parameters that are clearly defined. I like making a garden in an urban setting; the juxtaposition of shapes, the lobbying for light and nutrients, the negotiation with fences and buildings and sidewalks and hydro poles and trees a hundred years old.

Tito Mike starts by building cedar beds against the fences; two low, narrow beds, twelve feet in length. We repurpose the flagstone, laying it at the base of the beds to create walkways to stand on while planting. And then we tackle the bricks. We load them into a garbage bin on wheels in lieu of a wheelbarrow, pulling them out to the front of the house and stacking them on the sidewalk. Less than four hours later, an elderly Chinese couple comes by with a bundle buggy and looks for us to nod in encouragement. They make two dozen trips—her pulling the bundle buggy, him stacking bricks on a carrier on his ten-speed—taking away hundreds of bricks. We will later recognize them in the front yard of a triplex down the street, framing small plots of bok choy and onions and garlic.

"Chinese like that," says Tita approvingly. "Nothing waste."

Next we have to excavate the foot of sand and the foot

of gravel that underlies the bricks. No wonder the rain had simply puddled here. Digging it out is a huge project. Tita comes outside wearing winter boots and yellow rubber gloves. "Not in your job description," I say. She waves her gloved hand dismissively and starts shovelling sand into the garbage bin.

Tito Mike digs a trench from the back of the house to the fence and puts in weeping tiles. Then we begin moving the three cubic yards of topsoil I've had delivered from the laneway into the backyard. We fill in the yard garbage bin by garbage bin. It takes two days in the rain.

My brother helps me plant two Korean lilacs and three bridal wreath spireas against the back fence. In one of the beds, I plant lettuce and basil. "When we harvest, Mum?" Tita asks.

We spread grass seed, mostly fescue, between the beds. The shade dictates. I am thinking of my daughter, toddling and tumbling, hoping to create a lawn she'll encounter with her feet next summer. In the other bed, I plant a sandcherry, variegated sedum, barberry, deep purple flowering sage, white-flowering catmint, chokeberry, "Husker Red" penstemon, painted ferns. Back here, north-facing, it is a palette of purple, maroon, red, white and green. Pinks, oranges and yellows are strictly at the sunny south-facing front of the house—itself a considerable project undertaken with Tito Mike's help. He builds a raised cedar bed against the porch, which I plant with Japanese grasses and Russian sage. In the ground below I plant lavender, irises, delphiniums, butter-fly bushes, mock orange.

We're sitting on the front porch admiring our work one morning when Tito Mike points up and says, "What the fuck's wrong with that bird?" For weeks a robin has been attempting to build a nest in a corner under the eaves. It has no apparent talent; every day we sweep twigs, bark and straw off the front steps. "It's too late in the season," my brother says. "It's not going to lay eggs now. It's probably gay."

"It's the house where orphans come to roost," I tell him.

Word must be getting around.

II

In anticipation of moving out West, my brother has been asking questions about our father. He wonders if he might look him up en route across the country. He will leave us, his new-found family, and seek out the remnants of the old. We are each compelled by some need to put it all together, house the idea of family in a single frame. We remain hopeful, despite all evidence to suggest there is no reason to be. I have wondered sometimes whether *hope* is simply the human word for the animal impulse in us to survive.

I haven't wanted to point out the obvious to my brother, but twenty-two years ago, after our father had alienated everyone he knew and exhausted all possibilities here, he abandoned the meagre belongings of his life and set off for Vancouver. He didn't tell us this is what he was doing; he simply disappeared from his last known address. Ara also went west. The men in my family run away, all of them bound for the same place, it seems—a city hidden behind distant mountains; a purgatory at the edge of the new world.

A cop my brother knows has offered to do a quick search for my father. The cop comes back with nothing: no record, no driver's licence, no trace. Same with the police in Calgary. He would be seventy years old now, assuming he's survived the decades of hard living. There really is only one likely conclusion. It's what I will tell my daughter, in any case.

12

Micah will be going west, while we will be heading east. We will be as far apart as it is possible to be in this country.

When Miles and I had first met, I had reminisced about a brief visit to her small island fifteen years ago, specifically about a place where I had jumped off a bridge into a river and floated on a current out to sea. Hundreds of feet out, I had looked back to see this infinitely long and lonely expanse of sand. It was the most beautiful beach I had ever seen, a beach to rival any in the world.

I had no recollection of where it was. Miles named the beach, showing it to me on a map. Before she was born, I had resolved to take my daughter there.

In July we leave Tito Mike and set off in my Jeep—Miles and me up front, Tita and the egg in the back—on a road trip that takes us three days. The last leg involves crossing the Confederation Bridge, twelve and a half kilometres over the Northumberland Strait between New Brunswick and Prince Edward Island. The steep clay cliffs of the south shore of the island come into view, glowing red in the late-afternoon sun.

An hour later we arrive at Miles's parents' house just outside Charlottetown. She jumps out of the car and bounds across the grass into the middle of the vegetable patch her father is planting, throwing herself into his arms. The lonely gay comes from somewhere. This is her family, her home. Tita bursts into tears.

Miles's mother unearths her grandsons' baby toys for my daughter. Miles's father teaches Tita how to drive the tractor. Both her parents have effortlessly taken to calling their daughter Miles. We eat potato salad and macaroni salad and cold roast beef for dinner. Miles's father was once the Island's minister of agriculture. He's an astute and impassioned politician. I tell him he should run for mayor of Charlottetown and he raises his eyebrows. They stay stuck there. From here on we will refer to him as The Mayor.

I think later about Tita's bursting into tears. I'm struck by an awareness that Miles and Tita share something I don't. They have both had to venture out alone, leaving their families and their islands for better opportunities elsewhere. I don't share their sense of longing for a place and people elsewhere.

Tita keeps a large cardboard box at the end of her bed, which she fills with bits and pieces to send back to the Philippines. It's full of my old clothes and baby clothes my daughter has outgrown. She sends dishes and soap and shampoo and toothpaste and condiments and chocolate and cookies. The box is called a *balik bayan*—a back-and-forth—although it travels only one way. The boxes Miles receives from her parents and sends to her siblings and nephews are called care packages.

Tita's application for permanent residency includes an application for her husband. They will be reunited in Toronto eventually, make a new life together there. Miles's trajectory will be different. She will make a family, as lone immigrants and gay people do, she will find them in the city, a chosen family. And right now we are that family. We are a family because of a baby girl.

13

We've settled into an Island rhythm: days at the beach, collecting driftwood, swimming, picnicking, roadside stops for ice cream, my daughter happy splashing in the water, eating sand, berries, corn.

We are three women and a baby in a tiny rented cottage; four women when my mother comes to visit for a week, bombing around together in my Jeep exploring the island, fantasizing about real estate, visiting lighthouses, antique shops and provincial parks, stopping for fish and chips. The weather is blustery and unpredictable, quickly changeable. We make the most of every moment.

Early one evening Tita and I are up to our ankles in mud at the end of our garden. Miles and the egg are digging in the sand on the shore. The sun is setting, and the tide is low, exposing the red mussel flats of the bay. Below the red surface, the sand is a primordial black, low in oxygen and reeking of sulphur. It will oxidize a silver ring in a second, stain your hands and feet, but we have cast aside our shoes and are raking through the thick mud with our hands, risking the pinch of rock crabs and the sting of jellyfish.

We've been at this for twenty minutes and I'm feeling discouraged. Miles abandoned the project before we even started. Nothing but empty shells picked clean by birds. But Tita, with her leggings rolled up over her knees, is stubborn and determined. She is praying: Jesus, please give me ten mussels. And Jesus appears to be listening. After fifteen minutes she unearths her first barnacle-encrusted shell. She raises her arms in victory. She's never collected mussels before—clams, yes, but never mussels. Her family's farm is nine kilometres away from the ocean. She used to skip school with her cousin and friends and head to the water. They would collect clams, which they ate raw, dipping them in vinegar and chilies and salt. She taught herself how to swim and stole mangoes from trees on the way home.

For Miles the beach was the place where you did everything for the first time. People stole cars and booze from their parents' houses, drove the back roads in the middle of the night to avoid the police, built fires of driftwood, lobster traps and tires, swam, drunk and naked, had sex and returned home, underpants full of sand.

"You had sex?" says Tita. "You didn't worry about your future, Miles?"

"Hell no," says Miles. "There was no future. That was it."

We scrub those mussels and steam them in wine, chopped tomatoes, onion, garlic and parsley. We miss Tito Mike: he'd love this Island supper. There is brown bread from the local bakery. A lot of butter. We eat before the sun goes down, and go to bed shortly after, all of us on egg time. Eat/sleep/play, eat/sleep/play.

Tito Mike sends a text tonight as if he has heard us. "I miss you guys so much," he says. "That gay robin has finally built himself a nest."

14

Tito Mike has waited for our return. He has the remnants of a little blue shell to show me. The gay robin had laid a single egg, hatched it, then gone off, presumably in search of a bigger nest. Now Tito Mike is ready to move out West and Tita is packing a suitcase for the Philippines, going home for a month to see her family.

"Next time, we're coming with you," I say to Tita.

"Yeah, right," she says, rolling her eyes.

"I wish you didn't have to go," I say to my brother.

"Oh, Min," he sighs. "Why can't you just enjoy it for what it is?"

I'm trying to hold on to something that neither of them quite believes in, wants or needs in the way that

I do. I don't want my daughter to lose her uncle. I don't want to lose my brother. We had our first Christmas together as a family in fourteen years. I want Tita to come back before she has even left. I don't want to lose this sense of family that has surrounded us both for much of her first year. We celebrated all of our birthdays this year in this house. Tita turned thirty, Miles thirty-three, my brother forty-one, me forty-three. The egg will soon turn one.

We're having a final supper, sending them off with spaghetti and meatballs. Tita, watching my daughter's delight in flinging a meatball overboard, says: "I don't believe now that a pregnant mother's mood affects the baby." It's an Asian belief she'd held on to, one that my daughter's constitution seems to dispel.

Lolo, my stepfather, drives Tita to the airport early in the morning. I cry to see her go; my daughter has only once been apart from Tita for more than a weekend and I have not been a mother for any real stretch of time without Tita. Relief is on its way to the Philippines.

My stepfather stuffs a twenty-dollar bill into Tita's hand and tells her to buy something to eat during the layover in Hong Kong. "Like a real father," Tita texts me after checking in. "He make me cry!"

Two days later it's Tito Mike's turn. He has sold his truck and his hunting rifles. The old Volvo I gave him in exchange for renovating the basement is packed, two Muskoka chairs strapped to the roof.

He doesn't drag out the goodbye.

"Are you sure you'll be safe?" I ask through the window.

"Min, I could find drugs anywhere," he says, annoyed by the question.

But Vancouver isn't just anywhere. For all its gloss and glorious scenery, Vancouver is the last stop for many, and not just because it doesn't have the punishing cold of the rest of Canada. When you have drifted from place to place, you suddenly find yourself at the edge of the continent. There is nowhere left to go.

Vancouver has a side to it I haven't seen elsewhere. Micah will live within spitting distance of the Downtown Eastside, a neighbourhood where many people lie on the street, shooting up on the sidewalk. The city started the first needle exchange in North America there. The neighbourhood houses the first supervised injection site, serving hundreds of users a day.

Micah assures me that all that is behind him. He's free of drugs now—the methadone, even the prescription pills. He tells me he has never felt more supported and accepted than during this past year with us. But then, he doesn't expect very much. When I clipped a coupon from a magazine for him a couple of months ago he told me that it made him feel so loved. Two Big Macs for the price of one. Like the twenty dollars stuffed into Tita's hand.

My brother puts the car in drive and lights a smoke. He honks the horn as he pulls away. I have a terrible feeling I might be losing him for good, that my little girl will never know her uncle, he who was such an important part of her first year. In my experience, the men who set off for Vancouver never return.

The egg has been subdued since Tita left a couple of days ago, clinging to me in a way she hasn't before. First signs of separation anxiety. Perhaps she's picking up something from me.

part four

flight

I

It's so hot now, this August, that I have taken to lying on the basement floor. There are stretches, hours long, when I'm alone—Micah out West, Tita in the Philippines, my daughter's visits with Anna growing longer as she gets older—completely alone for the first time in a year.

I lie here and I think about how all our lives can be read as histories of love. A cycle of fantasies, fulfillments, failures.

I am stuck on the failures, full of the sense of endings. In my life I have dismissed, disappeared, drifted, detonated. And I have been ditched, outgrown, unrequited, abandoned.

Until a year and a half ago, I had some sense of what the rest of my life might look like. There is no longer a map. It's not a question of finding my feet, but of growing new ones. Trying to be a parent, teach a child how to be in the world, when I have lost the way.

It is easier (and certainly more presumptuous) to imagine the futures of others. Tita will be reunited with her husband, I assume Miles will find a partner one day, even if she is less optimistic about this than I am, and the egg will grow up and away from me. My brother asked me why I couldn't just enjoy our time together for what it was. He recognized the impermanence of our domestic arrangement, its transience.

We have not done well with families. Micah was married once. For three weeks. And yet, he still harbours a white-picket-fence fantasy.

I find myself thinking about a woman I used to know, a woman who loved me well before I was ready to be loved well. I have always wondered if we were somehow fated to be together. But then, I behaved very badly. Why she would ever trust me again, I cannot imagine.

I think about a younger man I barely know. A man who told me about his trip to New Zealand. I fantasize about moving there with him, spending six months a year in Canada renovating an old monster of a house, six months on the South Island with my hands deep in the antipodean earth. But his girlfriend wouldn't like it very much.

I think about a woman I met on holiday in Costa

Rica years ago. She had served in the Gulf War. I'd never met anyone who'd been in the military. She had paid for university by joining the reserves and never expected to be called up. She lived in the southern States and her home had been destroyed by a hurricane. All her poetry had been blown away. She spent months combing the wetlands, picking up loose-leaf sheets and photographs. She had the most beautiful face.

I think about Ted, with whom I still talk in my head sometimes.

I think about David, who I eventually discovered had left me while I was in Cairo for an academic in California. Still, I called him once I had finished my PhD, to thank him for having set me on an academic path. And then I told him he was shit.

I think about Hassan, who has remained in my life. We have written to each other for the past nineteen years. On thin blue airmail paper for the first few; then email, once access arrived in Ethiopia at the turn of the century.

Hassan has become more religious over the years, having made the pilgrimage to Mecca shortly after I left, though he has always treated the developments in my life, including my marriage, with the same open-minded spirit he possessed as a young man. We speak to each other much more openly than his culture would permit. We found, early on, our own language somewhere half-way in between.

I have never stopped thinking about Biscutti. After several years, though, I did stop asking Hassan about her. She would be in her twenties now. All Hassan would ever tell me was that she hadn't developed normally. He comes from a culture of optimism, where no one wants to be the bearer of bad news, not even a doctor.

Hassan has become a father. He married a cousin living in the United States quite a few years ago and they have two children, both of them U.S. citizens. Yet he remained in Ethiopia, despite having won that scholarship to study in America all those years ago. He was and will always be denied entry to the States. His future was completely rerouted because of an omission he made on his visa application. And then 9/11 happened. And his name is . . . well.

He treats his fate as a blessing, though, one that has allowed him to become a devoted doctor to his own people, greatly needed in a country where there is only one doctor for every forty thousand people. He has come to specialize in hematology, making him one of only two hematologists in the entire country.

It has been hard not to fantasize, at times, about the child he and I might have had together.

I entertain various fantasies, try them on, hoping to find out where, and with whom, I might fit. I am trying to relocate myself in love, looking for another to give my life shape.

2

I have a position as writer-in-residence at the university this fall. I ride my bike to campus on chilly fall
mornings, take a streetcar if it rains. It takes twenty-five
minutes either way; the first twenty spent missing my
daughter, the last five trying to remind myself that I
write for a living.

I ensconce myself in an old sloped-roof office with
water-damaged walls. I flick on my desk lamp and
stare out the window at the green quadrangle and cop-
per roofs of the college. It is comforting here, with
colleagues likewise ensconced, phones ringing down
the hall, pipes gurgling, a view of a quadrangle I know
so well.

I look out the window, into that quadrangle where a man once asked me why I was unhappy and gave me six thousand dollars to try to fix that.

I realize in that moment that some things can only happen when you are young and have nothing to lose. Now the answer to what's next is unlikely to be, or to be provided by, another person. If this were fiction I'd introduce a stranger at just this point in the story. But that would be a cheat, wouldn't it. The truth is, our stories unfold in less dramatic ways, the transformations that occur are incremental, less governed by happenings in plot than by shifts in feeling.

I try to imagine what a life lived without a partner would look like. I think of the adventures my daughter and I will have, the bike rides and kayaking and camping. Of the shared meals, midnight swims, cuddles and stargazing and sleep. Of the different parts of the world we will experience together. I remind myself of the privilege of our lives.

At Easter, we went to Spain with Tamzin and her beautiful children. Louie and Little Lulu, long and lean and blond—the girl Tamzin and I joke is responsible for the fact that I now have a child. We sat on mountainside terraces in Andalucía, gazed at the stars, drank Rioja and ate tapas, while her kids ran around the table and took turns carrying the baby. The baby ate olives and lamb and Manchego cheese. We followed an Easter procession through the late streets of

Grenada, walked the cobblestoned roads of mountain villages, played in the sun and the sand and the sea.

This summer I took the egg kayaking in the Northumberland Strait. We bicycled through shady ravines in the city. We visited friends on Lake Huron, where we bobbed together in the chalky waves. We spent weekends with my parents in the country.

I can appreciate the beauty of these moments when I describe them, but I have little feeling of beauty inside me. I can create happy moments for us and I can know that they are happy. I am doing my best to give my daughter a good life, exposing and introducing her to diverse and interesting people and experiences. I am watching her, watching the world. I have spent so much of my life watching it from a distance. Now it seems I am twice removed.

I'm reluctant to call this depression, but the ongoing absence of my ability to write is by this point starting to read like a symptom of some serious, underlying disease. I was relieved of any significant depression for all the years I was with Anna. And I was full of words. I worry that my relationship with Anna just masked what is broken in me, what has never been fixed, what may never be fixable. The near decade with her is bookended by the darkest two periods of my life. Perhaps this is the real me, not the happier, healthier, more confident and outgoing person I felt myself to be with Anna. I have to find some way to endure myself. I have a child to live for. I have to write.

———

I feel deeply ashamed walking into Dr. P's office all these years later. I come to her as a failed person.

"You left analysis too early," Dr. P says.

"Is that it?" I ask. "Is it that simple?"

"Mmm-hmm," she nods.

This gives me some reason to hope. Perhaps a process of transformation had been under way in analysis, something that could possibly be resumed. But I cannot afford Dr. P. She was expensive back then—she is even more expensive now.

Dr. P refers me to Dr. B.

I enter psychoanalysis for the second time in my life.

3

I am describing a steel box the height of a building, the four corroded walls that surround me. I sleep in the rusty corners and spend my days pacing in semi-darkness from wall to wall. There is no food or water.

I am creating a picture of my internal world for Dr. B.

Being a psychoanalyst with a medical background, she introduces the idea of taking an antidepressant. I had taken the Celexa my GP had prescribed after my daughter was born for just a month. Dr. B's suggestion sends me catapulting back twenty years. I know the slippery slope that can begin with one pill. Prescriptions for drug upon drug, which blunt and bloat but do not relieve you of nihilism and anhedonia.

I see that potential, but I also see a very warm and courageous person before me, someone willing to share something of her own experience with depression. She takes a pill every day. She doesn't imagine a day when she won't. She is humble and humane and honest and perhaps for no other reason in that moment than a desire to be humble and humane and honest like her, I will try.

It occurs to me later that I have written the story of this steel box before. In those early days of attempting to write short stories about people and places that mattered to me, I wrote a story about an African man in prison.

> For more than two years I existed in confinement so solitary that I began to forget myself. I lived in a three-by-three-foot cell with a piece of sky the size of a banana leaf one hundred feet above me. There was barely enough room for me to kneel, let alone lie down. Since I hadn't the strength to scale the walls, I clung like a silverfish to the dank, mildewed cement.

There is that tiny prick of light that Ian Brown described. A piece of sky the size of a banana leaf one hundred feet above.

I tell Dr. B about that piece of sky. She leans over

the steel box, this prison, to look inside it. She can see me there. I can see her. She is not hazy. She can hear me. And she is looking straight into my eyes.

4

Tita takes my daughter to the drop-in centre at a local school. It's a busy kaleidoscope of white, Chinese, Japanese, Indian and African kids and mums, and a good number of Filipina nannies. My daughter makes friends and so does Tita. Both of them suddenly have a social life, with play dates and potlucks and picnics and trips to the mall, all quite separate from me. They clear out the furniture from our living room so that five nannies and eight children can play. The nannies cook pancet and adobo. Their largely blond, blue-eyed charges tuck into Filipino food.

My daughter spends more time with her nanny now. I feel I have become more of an employer to her with this shift.

And now the nanny is mad at her employer. I've misplaced a necklace. I misplace everything these days. When I ask Tita if she has seen it, she hears an accusation. She bursts into tears, and I hate myself for even having mentioned it. It's no different to me than misplacing my keys, but I have no doubt there is a fine tradition of employers suspecting their nannies of stealing. "I realize this is a sensitive issue, Tita, but please trust me, you know me, I'm not accusing you." But she will not be reassured.

"I don't want to lose my job," she sobs.

In that moment I don't know what I can say to reassure her. For all the trust I thought we'd established, for all the intimacy of the past year, she seems not to know me. Doesn't she understand her power in this situation? Her value to me? She takes care of the thing that is most precious of all to me. In fact, I don't even know, don't even want to know what it would be like to have to raise my daughter without her.

"Why I work for you if you don't trust me?" she says angrily.

Is it really this tenuous? I don't feel it is, but then I am not the one in the vulnerable position. I might be dependent on her in many ways, but my livelihood is not one of them. Her work permit binds her to me, but the reverse is not true.

"I'll find the necklace," Tita says, and turns away from me. She disappears into her room.

I sit at the kitchen table and pour myself a giant glass of red wine. Early on I was aware that Tita's presence would have a significance for us that would outweigh ours for her. Perhaps that's why I want to make some kind of difference in her life. I think about the fact that I have made promises to Tita that speak to my desire to connect us in some lasting way. I have told her we'll take a *balik bayan* to the Philippines next year ourselves, travel to her small island and stay with her family on their farm. I've said Nico can live with us when he finally gets here if they are not in a position to afford their own place. I will help her go back to school if that is what she wants to do. The nascent future I envision includes her.

But perhaps Tita, Micah and I are even more alike than I had realized. I suspect we can all be domesticated by love, but when love is threatened or broken, our suspicions and mistrust are confirmed. Experience has made us this way. Perhaps she simply does not believe my promises that speak of permanence because the disappointment, if I fail to deliver, would just be too much.

It makes me wonder if this, in part, is why Micah had to run away. Because if you believe in what's promised, if you become invested, you take the risk of a broken heart.

I miss Micah, tonight more than most. One of the things I miss is the time we spent talking, filling in the gaps for each other. We didn't grow up in a house of stories. There was much my mother likely had to bury for our protection, and the stories my father told made less and less sense. I can count on one hand the stories I know about my mother's childhood. I have no idea how my parents met, or whether she was attracted to him. There were proposals before my father. Why him? I remember asking once. Her answer, nothing more than: I was twenty-six. It was time.

After becoming engaged, my mother embarked on the most mysterious chapter of her career with MI5. She went to Trinidad for two years in the mid-1960s, leaving her fiancé behind. Predictably enough, she will tell us nothing about what she was doing there.

We have become, as so many children do, excavators in the next generation. As we fill in the bits and pieces for each other, the authorship becomes shared and the stories altered, embellished, bettered perhaps.

Stories become shared in marriages, too. You can be so familiar with your spouse's family stories, so well acquainted with its characters that you begin to think of those stories as your own. It's what we do together—build a common history. Anna and I separated our furniture and the books and CDs and photographs, but the stories are so much harder to disentangle. It's one of the things I find saddest about the end of my marriage.

My ex-father-in-law died quite suddenly late last year. He was a man I loved and respected and had known not just for the duration of my marriage but for a lifetime in a way—through Anna's stories about him. He was a man of the world. He gave me an atlas one Christmas—the biggest and best atlas there is. I spend hours with it, much as I did poring over my father's atlas when I was a child. I miss him. I feel his absence more than I do that of my own father.

I can't afford to lose any more people. Come home, I say to my brother via text—the only way he'll communicate, the cheapest way. The job he'd lined up in advance hasn't worked out. Within his first three weeks in Vancouver he has used heroin again. He's back on methadone after all those painful months spent weaning himself off. After the methadone, the OxyContin, the Tylenol 3s. He swears he never shared needles, but he has just been diagnosed with hepatitis C. He has gum disease. His body is breaking down as a result of all the years of abuse.

You cannot be a drug addict at forty. You can be dead. Fuck, Micah, come home.

But what do I even mean by that? Come home to my house? Bring your big messy self back into the fold? My baby is no longer such a baby. She is very much aware.

And my house is not the cozy and accommodating bubble it once was. It's a mix of people with individual needs that can't always be met within these walls.

The fight between Tita and me seems to have suddenly reduced our relationship to simply one between employer and employee. I can't believe that it can be so easily stripped of all its layers and complexity. It can't for me. I will keep my promises. I will prove to her that this has more substance and depth; that *I* do.

I know her in ways that transcend our employment relationship. I know her as moral and strong-willed, open-minded, mischievous, sarcastic, moody, irreverent, adventurous, artistically and musically talented, shrewdly attuned to people, uncannily wise to what makes them tick. And I know some of the stories of the formative moments in her life. I know, for instance, that the night after her wedding, all of her jewellery was stolen from her house. The house was under construction. There were bars on the windows, but no glass. They had entertained the entire village that day. Most of the villagers are also relatives. Lots of people stayed over, sleeping on bamboo mats outside. Hands reached through the bars in the night.

She has not felt the same way about the village since. With that violation it ceased, in fact, to be home.

The morning after our impasse, Tita and I are polite, but the cloud lingers. I break the silence and ask again where I went wrong. She is willing to tell me now that despite my denials, there was something in my tone that she did take to be accusatory. I apologize, I grovel, I am practically on my knees. She cries, I cry. She hugs me, I hug her.

"Do you think it reminds you of when your own jewellery was stolen?" I venture.

"There might be a connection," she says, picking up a crumb off the table with her finger.

"Ah," I say. "Who's the resident psychologist now?"

She smacks me gently on the forearm.

5

After a very bad start in Vancouver, Micah has managed to pick himself up. He's in a methadone program again and taking interferon for the hepatitis, fortunately an easily treated strain. He's found himself a job working for a condo developer with fifty years of projects ahead of him. He has also changed his name.

Our father did the same thing, several times in fact. I had given the private detective I hired to find him, thirteen years after he disappeared, a number of different names. He had spent his last years in Ontario living as someone else.

"Nice new business card," my mother (ever a precise proofreader) compliments my brother (a dyslexic speller at best), "though you've misspelled both your first and last names."

"It's my new persona," my brother says.

Miles has moved to the city. She has an apartment nearby, so close that I can take the baby out in her stroller and meet her for coffee. We often spend the weekend together, living a life that revolves around a baby. We take her to nearby parks and paddling pools, go for bike rides, my daughter in her seat on the back. On Saturday mornings we go to the farmers' market, where my baby girl keenly samples artisanal cheeses and sausages.

We are not a couple, even though we must appear to the world as if we are. I love Miles; she is a gift in all our lives—a friend and a sister and an important part of my daughter's life—but she is not my lover or a parent. There are times when we look like a family—my daughter careening between us, holding both of our hands—times where I unwittingly step outside the moment and become conscious of what this is not. It can take some of the happy out of the happy moments.

In the absence of both Miles and Tita, I remain daunted by the hours with my baby. The entertainment, the patience, the repetition, the boredom, the isolation. I distract the egg with outings as best as I can, but on weekends, seeing other couples with their children, other people being normal families, I feel the sadness welling up in me. I am afraid of time alone with my daughter in large part because of the anticipation, the expectation that I should be experiencing joy when what I experience is the conspicuousness of its absence. That makes me feel like a terrible mother.

It is easier to be on the move or to be surrounded by others than to face both the reality of mothering and my fear of it.

On my own, I can imagine only water. I knew my daughter would be a swimmer long before she was born. I took her into the bath with me the day after she was born and have been swimming with her from the time she was three weeks old. She had swum in the waters of Lake Ontario, Lake Huron, the Mediterranean and the Atlantic before she was even a year old.

In my one fantasy of the future she is on water. I am driving her long, lean, petulant self down to Lake Ontario in the dark early mornings to rowing practice. She is fourteen. She slams the door of the car and makes her way from the parking lot down to the lake. I stay in my car, drinking tea, reading the newspaper, loving her despite her disdain.

6

In the new year, having waited nineteen months, Tita finally gets preliminary approval of her application for permanent residency. The process of sponsoring Nico can now begin, and she has the freedom now to make some choices. Her work permit is no longer tied to a specific employer and she is no longer obliged to be a live-in caregiver. She is free to choose where she lives and works, how much she works and for whom.

Free and not. Living elsewhere, alone or in an apartment shared with friends, costs money. So does taking courses. A family gets used to receiving a certain amount in remittances—in fact, the economy of the Philippines would collapse without them. It's hard to reduce that amount, making the case for short-term cutbacks as an investment in bigger, longer-term rewards, especially when people back home are hungry. Ten people back home are dependent upon Tita.

But what work is she going to do if she doesn't have some further training? She is not uneducated. She has a university degree. But without some specific schooling here it won't get her anywhere. She knows that. "I can work at Tim Hortons for minimum wage," she says. Less money than she makes now. "Then I have to pay my rent." And then there is nothing left. Nothing left to send home or save for a house or go back to school or raise children. She's met women who have returned to caregiving after stints at coffee shops. Women who have gone back to living-in. Many Filipinas remain as caregivers for the rest of their lives.

If Tita and Nico could live with me, she could go back to school and work part-time for me in lieu of rent until she is working full-time elsewhere. If she lived with us, my daughter would continue to have access to her Tita. She doesn't know a life without her. But this would require my finding a bigger house. If there was a separate apartment, perhaps Miles could rent it until Nico arrives. She is with us much of the time as it is. My daughter would have a playmate in residence, I would have a friend. It would have to be a big enough house for Micah to stay in as well if he wanted or needed to. And while I'm at it: with enough room for Lolo and Lola in their later years.

When I last looked for a house, just two years ago, I simply looked for somewhere that felt safe for me as a single pregnant woman, somewhere for me and my unborn child to land. There was urgency to the decision, a desperate need for containment at a time when I could not have felt more vulnerable and uncertain. There was no Tita then, no Micah, no Miles. My parents weren't with us for dinner twice a week. There wasn't even a baby. But while I knew she would arrive, I couldn't see the others coming. I couldn't imagine that I would soon find myself in a house populated, and at times overrun, by a family.

The house I am looking for now needs to be big enough not just to contain us but to afford us all a little privacy. We clung to each other in the first house; now we all need the room to grow. I need the room, both physically and psychically, to entertain new possibilities. What if I were to meet someone? What if there were to be another child—someone else's or even my own? I have a fantasy of a house that could be a home for even those I have yet to imagine.

7

I am keeping my promises to Tita. We are in the Philippines with her family for a month. She lives in my place, and now my daughter and I are experiencing something of hers. We're bridging the gaps between us in all the ways I know how.

My daughter is feeding the chickens, having taken this on as her job under Tita's mother's direction. She is playing ball with Tita's nieces, picking up Visayan words, swimming naked in the sea. I am getting to know Tita's parents and siblings and, more importantly, Nico. He is a beautiful man, both physically and temperamentally—a gentle soul, a devout Catholic, a dedicated son to a mother of thirteen children. My daughter calls Nico

Tutu. Tata and Tutu. I call them the Brangelina of Bohol.

This trip is an investment in a shared future. Theirs and ours. Their future, Tita's and Nico's and the children they will eventually have, is not here. I understand why she had to leave; it's not a big or complicated mystery. Life here is tough. It is all subsistence farming, with little prospect of getting beyond that. The work is relentless, and the result of all that labour? Rice on the table. With a bad harvest, not even that.

We talk as much about Toronto while we are here as we do about what is going on around us. My real estate agent is forwarding me listings. Among them is what might be the right house. I show it to Tita before forwarding it to my mother back in Toronto. My mother goes to see the house for me. There is not enough of a signal here for me to view a virtual tour. My mother loves the house and she knows I will love it too, and so I buy a house over the internet. The details of the offer are negotiated via Facebook chat between an office in Toronto and a bamboo-roofed internet café on an island in the middle of the Visayan Sea. It's a snowy February night there, a hot and humid February morning here.

I make a great leap of faith over a lot of distance. And I've just spent a lot of money. There will be no more travelling for a good long while. It is time to stop running, time to settle down.

I show Tutu photos of the house where we will all live, including, in the not-too-distant future, him. "Thank you for trusting my wife," Tutu says. "Thank you for your good heart."

Tutu's limited English forces us both to speak plainly. "I love Tita," I tell him. "She's my family. And that means you are, too."

8

We have moved into our new house in the middle of the city. The new house is actually a rambling old house with rambling-old-house problems. It's daunting—both the financial fact of taking on this house on my own, and the work it requires. I miss my brother, his enthusiasm for such projects and his handy ways. I am loathe to tell him we have moved from the house that he was such a part of making into a home. Here, I must start again.

First off, the electricals need replacing; all the knob-and-tube wiring has to be torn out, just as in the old house. I hire the same electrician I hired two years ago, more for sentimental reasons than anything. His assist-ant, a Ugandan man whose own children are back home in Kampala until he can afford to sponsor them, looks me up and down when I open the door. He's never seen me un-pregnant. He takes in my girl, no longer a baby.

"Isn't God great," he says, shaking his head.

He and his boss are kind men, both fathers. My daughter calls them "man" and "two man" respectively. She fills their toolbox with broken chalk and shells.

Once the electricals have been replaced, Miles and I replaster patches of wall and paint most of the house with the help of a couple of friends. Miles will move in at the end of the month. I do not yet have a separate apartment—that will have to be built—so in the meantime, she'll take the big front bedroom on the second floor. I worry a bit that privacy—hers and mine—will be an issue, whether we'll each have the room for independent lives, what will happen if either of us begins to date. I hope we'll find a way to talk about such things; I cannot say it comes naturally to either of us.

There is work to distract us in the meantime. We fix a leaking radiator, then replaster a ceiling damaged by said leaking radiator. We learn how to force reluctant water through the radiator system so there is heat on the third floor. We replace a downspout from an eavestrough. We dig three-hundred-pound boulders out of the dirt in the backyard by putting all our weight onto the handles of two spades and rolling them onto a tarp. We take instructions from elderly Portuguese neighbours and videos on YouTube.

Our neighbourhood is busier, and so are we. Tita takes the egg to a new drop-in school, and there they make a wider and more diverse circle of friends. It's a longer walk, with many more distractions along the way. Miles is busy with her thesis. She has a deadline and she's determined to reach it. She writes in a coffee shop for several hours every day, then gives her brain a break, watching horror films on her laptop in the late afternoon.

I am teaching but still failing to write. During my sessions with Dr. B, I talk about the writer I used to be when I was young and life was full of chaos and tumult. It was intense, instinct-driven, risk-taking, passionate and often painful, and that was reflected in my writing. I wrote letters and journals, fiction and non. I wrote to communicate with people, for purposes of comfort or relief or rebellion, to work out something complicated or because language had taken hold of me and simply demanded a paragraph, a poem be written.

Writing once fulfilled so many needs that could not otherwise be met. I am bereft without it, particularly when it could serve me in the very essential way it has done for most of my life.

Dr. B says that I can write to her. That generosity cracks open my chest. It touches that place underneath where all the feelings that have yet to be put into words are trapped. Somewhere between sternum and diaphragm; a place very raw, very red.

Soon enough, words are pouring out, two winters' worth of ice thawing overnight: the grief and that tight knot of anger lodged in the pit of me becoming unstuck. Unmoored, though, they threaten to destroy everything. The feelings are bigger than me, stronger. I am afraid of their intensity; I am afraid of going crazy, of doing harm, of standing on a bridge plenty high enough, when this is no longer, if it ever even was, an option.

One witness, though—one reliable and loving witness with the capacity to hold—can change what you are convinced will be the inevitable outcome.

9

My friend Agitu comes for dinner with her daughters. We first met when she came to Toronto as a refugee over twenty years ago; now she is a social worker in California and the mother of two lovely and extremely articulate teenagers. It is our friendship that led me to Ethiopia. Her story of escape from her country, the stories of her brothers, all of whom spent time in prison, all of these things led me there. Agitu is part of who I am, indelible.

Over dinner, we are reminiscing about her first year in Canada. I have visited Agitu in California, but her daughters don't know this place, where their mother's new life began.

She says she spent much of her first year in Toronto

in a daze. She was plagued by nightmares, terrified of the police, startled by loud noises and thoroughly depressed by the Canadian winter. All these years later she has a name for what she was experiencing then: post-traumatic stress disorder.

"English allows you to talk about suffering," I remember her saying to me once. "It is shameful to do so in my language." I knew how true this was, having spent a year in Ethiopia by then; the number of young men I knew who had been imprisoned and tortured under the Mengistu regime, their bodies testament to this, who would say nothing about these years.

We had been at her kitchen table in Palo Alto, her daughters young, watching *Barney*, her husband, a man she had met in Addis as an undergraduate but been separated from for years, hunched over his computer. We were recording her life story. We were doing it for her and for her children. A long, unstructured interview that took place over two weeks. Tape after tape, which I transcribed when I got back to Toronto.

Being able to put your experiences into a narrative gives meaning to the life you have lived. It can allow you to make sense of the things that have seemed the most senseless and cruel by providing some context—even if that context is nothing more than: It didn't kill me. I am alive to tell this tale. I am here, where I was once there. There is a story, possibly a universal one, of the passage between there and here.

Agitu's visit tonight makes me think about all of this. I met her after returning from Egypt. I was a mess. Agitu was even more disoriented. Here we are now, twenty-four years later, talking as mothers. I cannot compare my experiences to hers, but I can say that for all the respective disruptions we have experienced in our lives, there is this one simple certainty: we will be mothers for the rest of our lives, because of these girls, our daughters.

Agitu leaves a present for my daughter long after she has gone to bed, a white monkey with big blue eyes. It feels wrong somehow—a white monkey with blue eyes from a black woman from Africa—but then I remember the stories Agitu used to tell me about growing up at the foot of a mountain, where the colobus monkeys used to call out in the night, her love for them and the nature that surrounded them.

My daughter explodes with excitement when she sees the white monkey in the morning. She calls it Magitu and clasps it to her chest.

10

Grief is the overwhelming result of so many compounded losses that it is impossible to process as a whole. So you don't. You spend a thousand hours in therapy talking about the thousand things that hurt, one by one, in excruciating detail. That mass of grief holds the loss of the person you loved, the idea of them, the person you were with them, the life you shared, the friends and community and extended family you shared, the idea of who you were together—it challenges the very idea of your life and yourself.

And it collapses time: the present, the future and the past. It has the effect of a stone thrown into water. The stone descends, plummets through your past, stirring up all the associations that inform your experience of the present. This grief you experience in the present is a giant that has been fed by all past losses—the unexplained departures, the abrupt endings, the lack of resolution, the things that have gone unmourned for reasons of stoicism or denial or anger or inexplicability.

And while it plunges you into the past, the splash above radiates in ripples, travelling farther than the eye can see. It encompasses things far beyond the known, swallowing up all the possibilities one has yet to even consider. It has a way of erasing the future before you've even dreamt it.

I would have tried to conceive another child some time ago if my circumstances had been different. I can't pinpoint the moment that desire started: it feels like it has always been there, perhaps buried under the mountain of grief, perhaps even a good part of the grief without my being aware of it; that loss of what you have even yet to imagine.

I was certainly aware of the sadness I felt in March around what would have been my first baby's second birthday. I think of him as my lost child. I wish I could recover that loss. That loss that might have been the miscarriage of my marriage as well. I wish, somehow, I could begin again, at least begin with the awareness that I am doing this on my own. Of my own choice.

Tita senses my preoccupation and asks me what's up.

"Just do it, Mum," she encourages me.

"But I don't think I could do it without you."

"Don't worry, Mum," she says. "I will be with you."

"No, Tita, you're not going to be a nanny forever."

She has her own ambitions. She's been thinking about going back to school for early childhood education. Working in a daycare. Perhaps starting a daycare of her own.

It would seem I need only the slightest bit of encouragement, though. I lost my partner, not my ovaries. I find myself making an appointment to see the fertility doctor. Just to ask her if I'm insane.

It doesn't seem so long ago that I was spending five or six dark mornings of every month awaiting my turn at this clinic. In one line to have a needle poked into a bruised arm, in a second line to have an ultrasound to measure the swollen follicles, the burgeoning egg. That waiting room, the air full of a hundred unspoken stories: tales of failure and frustration, desperation and desire. Women of every hue. And several men.

Hormones, eggs and sperm were all that mattered here, not the you and your story. I felt the quiet pain in the room. No one spoke. Everyone avoided eye contact. No one wanted to be seen. Chances were you would see someone you knew.

I did sneak a few furtive glances. I wanted to know whether I was old, too old to be doing this. And now I'm even older.

I asked my mother what she thought of the idea of my having another child.

"You'd be making life very difficult for yourself," she said, speaking from experience and never being one to spare me. I am, to my detriment perhaps, rather more romantic.

"Am I insane?" I ask the doctor.

"Possibly," she says, "but let's check it out."

And so once again I'm waiting to have blood drawn and an ultrasound. I'm on my own in this room in the early morning as I was always on my own in this room in the early morning. I never asked Anna to come. I thought it was unnecessary for us both to have to get up so early in the morning, and left her to sleep. Being in the room this time is an entirely different experience. There isn't someone who could be here with me. It is a small difference with huge significance. I feel light, optimistic. I don't feel pain in this room. Everyone here must be possessed with hope. They wouldn't be here otherwise.

The test results are all normal. Some part of me had hoped my body would relieve me of having to make a decision. It may still relieve me, but for now the choice to proceed or not is mine. In all likelihood I won't be able to conceive or hold on to what might be conceived. I'm not interested in any kind of fertility treatment or intervention.

Perhaps I am simply here in this room in order to

rewrite the story. To make it my own, regardless of the outcome. Perhaps I am simply here in search of an end.

I I

My mother has accompanied my daughter and me to a writers' festival on the West Coast. We're spending a night in Vancouver so we can see Micah and Ara. Lolo is taking Tita and Miles out for sushi tonight in Toronto, while we will be having dinner at my brother's apartment. This will be the first time Ara, my mother, my brother and I have all been together in thirty years.

My mother is having a wardrobe crisis. We are in our hotel room getting ready and she's asking me if she looks fat. She is seventy-three years old and has never been fat in her life.

We take a taxi to Micah's apartment. He is waiting outside, smoking a cigarette, hanging with his dog, the

Frenchie who is the new love of his life. He looks good: he looks healthy and happy. He is even-tempered and his hep C treatment is working. He's wearing shorts and sandals. I haven't seen him in anything but jeans and boots since he was a kid.

Ara is there, too, smoking and leaning against a brick wall, looking like a tanned and shaggy-haired old hipster. "Holy crap" is the first thing he says when he sees us getting out of the cab. "Can you fucking believe this?" is the second, as Micah leads us up to the second floor of his apartment building. The dimly lit hall is half a mile long and smells of old dog and decades of smoke. Renting here apparently doesn't require a credit check.

He has a good-sized if rundown apartment with a view of the railway tracks and the mountains beyond. Sunlight floods the rooms. My brother has the obligatory bachelor-black leather couch and giant-screen TV. He has planted runner beans and cabbage in window boxes hanging off a balcony the size of a single bed. He is on his knees, grilling a feast for us out there on a tiny butane-fed barbecue. Eggplant, peppers, onions, mushrooms, B.C. salmon, Alberta steak. He doesn't even drink a beer.

"What happened to your beautiful long hair?" Ara asks my mother as they sit down together on the couch.

"I cut it off thirty-three years ago," she says. "You were there."

They both laugh.

He is attached to an image that didn't even exist by the time he left. Perhaps we all do this to greater and lesser degrees. Perhaps we need to, in order to keep people with us. Dr. B has given me language for this. In the absence of someone, even someone who has caused you great injury, the very idea of them can still be self-sustaining. You hold on because you are holding on to something that keeps your sense of self intact. You have come to know and understand yourself in relation to this person. You can let go only when your sense of self, your cohesion, no longer depends upon the idea of them, an idea that remains for a long time inextricable from the very idea of yourself.

12

I tried for two months to have a baby. If I'd been younger and coupled, I would have tried longer and harder, but in my circumstances this was as far as I wanted to go. It gave me an answer, an ending I needed.

Perhaps it is only when enough individual losses are articulated and mourned that a sense of grief can really shift as a whole. The process that leads you there is cumulative, though largely imperceptible. Subtle indicators along the way are the only measure, but the shift itself I experienced as a single moment. I will even dare, at the risk of sounding New Agey and flaky, to say I saw it happen.

In the middle of the night, my three-year-old daughter asleep beside me in my bed clutching her monkey,

Magitu, a cloud of white particles appeared beyond the foot of the bed, shimmered in slivers of streetlight coming in through the wooden slats of the blinds and then dissipated. I am a skeptic by nature, and I've never experienced anything like this before. And yet I entirely trusted that it was real. I knew these white particles had come from me. I dared myself to breathe in deeply in order to test whether this expulsion was really physical: if it was, there should be much more room inside me. I inhaled deeply and inflated like a balloon.

It was the idea of the life I was supposed to have. It was everything that included the words *should be, supposed to*. Surrender those words and you are left with what is.

Grief is in no way a blessing. But in some way, working your way through it may offer an opportunity to mourn so many other things you have hitherto been unable to. Things that have kept you hurt or small or angry. Old things that have determined how you encounter the new.

13

My daughter is punching the iPod with a determined finger. At three, she has her own playlist. She tells me what to download. Her most recent addition? Katy Perry's "Roar."

"Dance!" she commands.

And so we dance, each of us uninhibited in our expression around this little girl, each of us better known to each other than we could ever be in her absence. She has made us who we are: tigers, champions, mothers, grandparents, uncles, aunts.

My parents leave. I put my tired daughter to bed in the big room at the front of the house that Miles occupied until a month ago. Miles and her partner, Teiya, and I drink the last of the wine and then I see them to the door with Tupperware full of leftovers. They live five minutes away: proximity to us being Miles's one condition when they were looking for a place. She is no longer a lonely gay. Teiya wants them to get a dog. Miles, almost thirty-six now, is leaning more toward the idea of a baby. My daughter thinks her baby should be called Birdy.

Tita and I are in the kitchen doing the dishes after everyone leaves. She has her own apartment downstairs, newly renovated, two bedrooms, one for her and her husband, one for their baby. She is six months pregnant, having conceived on her last trip home, and although they could not have predicted this at the time, Nico's arrival is now within sight.

I accompany Tita to her midwifery appointments, and my mother takes her to her ultrasounds. This baby will be part of our family. I will get the chance to enjoy a baby. And whatever name they choose to put down on the birth certificate, this baby will be known to us as Angel Cinderella. My daughter has picked up her Tita's fondness for bestowing nicknames.

I ask Tita if she is okay downstairs, whether she isn't lonely.

"I have been lonely for thirteen years, Mum," she says.

"Oh, Tita," I say, putting my arms around her.

"Thirteen Christmases on my own."

"Not the last three," I say, hopefully. "Not anymore."

"Can you imagine, Mum? Sitting in the Tim Hortons

on your own on Christmas Day. I don't want to look anywhere, because I look over here and this guy is talking to himself and this way someone is twitching around and if I look this way someone says: Can you spare some change? I want to yell at him: Do you know how hard I work for this coffee?

"But it's okay," she says. "I am in a better position than them. At least I am not crazy."

"You still have your mind," I say.

"I still have my mind," she repeats.

I picture my father later. I think of the stories behind these faces, of what led these men here. I wonder if my mother held on to that psychological assessment of my father that was done all those years ago. I wouldn't be surprised. She is a meticulous filer of all vital information. She is the keeper of secrets, after all.

14

Two weeks before Tita is due to give birth her husband arrives from the Philippines. It is the coldest winter in twenty years. I watch Nico take his first breath after the whoosh of the sliding glass doors at the airport opens to the parking lot. He looks startled by the sensation in his lungs. Everything, everything must be shocking to him, but there is no time to gently acclimatize. Tita takes him to Chinatown to show him where to buy rice, where to buy fish and fruit and vegetables. She takes him to various government offices to get his paperwork in order.

Nico has brought traditional herbs from Tita's mother. She squats over half a basketball in which the herbs are burning, bathing herself in their aromatic smoke. Nico rubs snake oil onto his wife's belly. Tita's mother killed the snake herself.

I am an anthropologist in my own house. The kind of anthropologist my supervisor long ago implied was to my detriment: immersed somewhere to such an extent that my sense of self was shattered by leaving.

But this time, this is my life. This is my house. This is my family. I have no life elsewhere to return to. I have no other home. I seek no other.

Tita goes into labour five days early. After twenty-four hours of slow contractions, the midwife arrives. Tita suddenly says she is ready to push. The midwife says that gives us just fifteen minutes to get to the hospital, and so we pack ourselves into her car. We don't even admit Tita, but take her straight up to a delivery room: the baby is on its way.

Tita lies down on the cot in a delivery room, and while the midwife is punching her name into a computer Tita gives one mighty push, and Nico and I can suddenly see a head. The midwife is snapping her gloves on, the backup midwife has yet to arrive, and Tita gives one more long and mighty push and that black-haired baby is born.

Tita didn't need any of us. She didn't need prenatal classes or someone holding her hand or pain relief. She carried a baby and gave birth with the same practical and efficient skill she applies to everything. She made it all look graceful, in fact.

Hello, Mama Tita. You are the strongest woman I have ever known.

And hello, Angel Cinderella. I am your Tita. Your *ate*—your big sister—is waiting at home.

15

Two dozen Filipino-Canadian babies are being baptized by an Indian priest in a small urban church. A street festival is happening outside; the steel drums of a calypso band underscore the proceedings, adding a certain surreality, and a levity I know will bother Tita. This is not her regular church—she prefers the Catholic church in our old neighbourhood because of the solemnity of its priest and its aged Chinese population. In all her years abroad, on her own, she has never surrounded herself with Filipinos, but this is both the church Tutu's cousins attend and a church that doesn't require godparents to have baptismal certificates. Miles and I, atheists of questionable orientation, are to be Angel's godparents. Tita and

Tutu are devoted Catholics, but *their* religion includes us.

Never having been to a christening, I had thought it was all about protecting the child from the devil. Only once I am standing there, Miles and I the tallest and whitest, in front of the pulpit, do I understand that they are ensuring their daughter's belonging in the house of God. That this is an act of communion, of community. That to raise a child with God is to protect her, in some senses, from the kind of existential loneliness that plagues some of us. Perhaps *that* is the devil.

My father used to quote Marx: religion is the opium of the people. There was nothing of the people about him. He condemned weakness, human reliance on religion or the state. It didn't leave my brother and me much room to consider a spiritual life or life as part of a community. We were raised not to belong.

At the christening my mother wordlessly hands me an envelope. I stuff it in my purse for later, knowing what it contains. She's found that profile of my father.

"Mr. Gibb's strong intellectual abilities are supported by an equally strong feeling of superiority," I later read. He is "so convinced of his problem-solving ability that he doesn't make use of a review mechanism that a more restrained, humble individual would normally use."

The psychologist goes on to characterize my father as "aggressive . . . restless and impatient to achieve a position of dominance," and says that "seeing himself as exceptionally bright and superior, he feels that life and other people should treat him that way. He is demanding, outspoken, sharp-witted and sharp-tongued; he makes use of humour, but in a biting, cynical, sarcastic way which, I feel, displays contempt for people."

There is more. "A self-sufficient loner . . . Mr. Gibb wants to run his own show with relatively little interference from others. He is apt to set very high standards and be quite intolerant of people who cannot live up to them. In assessing the motives of others, I find that he is overly suspicious and overly judgmental. In a supervisory role, I feel that he would be a cold, over-bearing dictator."

The report is dated November 1971, just three months after my mother, brother and I joined my father in Canada. I wonder how a psychologist would diagnose such a man today. The *DSM-II*, the edition of the diagnostic manual at the time, listed homosexuality as a mental disorder, but had no entries for any number of later-identified personality disorders that might have applied to my father.

Would a label have helped? I don't know. All I know is that there is no greater supervisory role than that of being a parent. And that there is no room for God when a man believes himself to be one.

I wonder, too, whether this psychologist could have predicted that Mr. Gibb would become a man so afraid of the world, of the people in it, that he would disappear.

As a consequence of my father's parenting, I find faith in God one of the most challenging of imaginative leaps. I have long envied people with that capacity. I have written characters whose faith is the most important thing in their lives. Since my daughter was born, I have gone to the Quaker meeting house on the occasional Sunday to sit in silence among others. I sit there simply as an invitation to possibility. As a reminder to keep my head and my heart open.

After Angel's christening, we're invited to a massive Filipino buffet at the home of one of Nico's cousins. Nico hands me a plate. "C," he says. "You are with us in everything."

16

It is spring, finally, late and long-awaited spring. On a Saturday morning, Tita and I pack our daughters into my car for the drive out to my parents' place in the country. Nico is riding ahead with my parents in their car, the first time he has left the city. He arrived in the dead of winter just three months ago and now he is a father to a baby eleven weeks old.

I imagine spring through Nico's eyes—the sudden and improbable burst of colour that erupts from barren ground and naked trees—seeing this transformation for the first time. Of learning the rhythms of this place, his daughter's country.

I remember how at seven and a half months pregnant

I'd gone kayaking alone on a cold Northern Ontario lake. The bulk of my belly had been awkward, but the rest of the ride was easy, effortless even—sublime. I remember looking at the shore, its dense wall of pines, a landscape that has always struck me as monotonous and unwelcoming, if not outright hostile. I could picture my child seated between my stomach and the paddles, taking it all in for the first time. I suddenly felt an acute awareness that this was her country, the landscape she would inherit: its water, its seasons, its sky, its pines. It was a visceral awareness, a felt understanding of place and belonging that had completely eluded me before.

After a mammoth lunch in the country, we fill the wading pool for my daughter. Lolo retires to watch golf, and Nico helps my mother out in the garden. He is a farmer, learning the names of new plants, how to distinguish nascent flowers from weeds. Tita plays with my daughter in the pool, her own daughter strapped into the BabyBjörn that I inherited from another writer and mother four years ago.

I am sitting in the shade of the porch, doing the crossword puzzle. It was over two years before I could resume doing the puzzle, three before I could take any real pleasure in it.

I look up at the scene in front of me, this tableau of people engaged in various tasks, all together in this particular place, in this exact moment, because of one little girl. She is at the heart of an even broader community of consistent and loving adults, adults flawed and damaged in the various ways so many adults are, all of them trying to raise a child with a healthy sense of herself. We are doing our best for her. She is the seed from which all this has grown.

My daughter chatters to her Tita. Nico saws the dead branches off an unruly juniper, stopping when he discovers a nest—four eggs of an impossible blue cradled in the undergrowth.

Doves are cooing in the background. The sound reminds me of England. In the garden of the house we lived in just before we left—Starlings, it was called, appropriately enough—my father kept doves and pigeons.

There are sounds and smells I have carried with me, more sensory than literal memories of the place I was born. I grew up in this country. I remember when we moved into the first house we owned, a lush August day in the early 1970s, when we ate Kentucky Fried Chicken in a backyard full of dandelions. It was a small wood-frame farmhouse circa 1900, with a big front porch and a sloping red roof. It needed a lot of work, but my father, who was not only without much money but arrogant and cheap, was fortunately also resourceful and talented.

There was a time when he put those talents to good use. The house needed rewiring, replumbing and reroofing. There was a crawl space of a basement, the house wasn't insulated, and the garden was a jungle. For the five years my father was with us we lived in a building site.

There was a perpetual film of sawdust on the floor, and there were always paintbrushes decomposing in stinking mason jars in the sink.

My brother and I loved living in a building site. My mother preferred the results to the process. My father eventually completed most of the major jobs, though we could always see our breath on winter mornings because the house never was insulated, and I thought it was perfectly normal to share a house with squirrels and raccoons, the skittering of their nails across the ceiling a source of comfort.

My father transformed our backyard—all 30 by 175 feet of it—adding a new back porch with steps down to a brick patio and a lawn, beyond which a stone path wound underneath a grape arbour suspended between a playhouse (where I had my first kiss) and a swing set he built for us. Past that there was a gardening shed (where I had my first cigarette) and two concrete-bound beds— one for vegetables (tomatoes, zucchini, squash), one for rhubarb and strawberries and fruit-bearing bushes (raspberry, gooseberry and redcurrant). Finally, a row of ferns lined the stone cemetery wall (the cemetery where I *almost* had sex for the first time).

I have a thousand stories to tell my daughter. And through those stories, I can reclaim some of the happier moments of my childhood. If I were to string those moments together, I could tell a very different story.

One day my daughter might tell someone that there

used to be peacocks in the cemetery, a small detail of family history she might choose to adopt as her own. Perhaps belonging lies in these sorts of details, their accumulation and continuity, the meanings we assign to them, the stories we pass on.

I have a job to do as a storyteller: we all do. To tell stories that make us knowable to others, most importantly our children. To give them the tools to help them know themselves. And perhaps we come to know ourselves differently as a consequence.

This is the circle that could never quite be complete. One where we are truly bound for better or worse, in all sorts of complex and beautiful ways, where we become ourselves in relation to each other and carry something of the other—visceral, embodied—within us. It is a story with a different ending. A story without an ending at all.

And this, I know, is happy.

postscript—august 2014

It is the end of a late-summer day and Micah and I are sitting on some rocks in the middle of a community garden near Vancouver's Downtown Eastside. This is where he comes to forage, for apples and blackberries, zucchini, tomatoes, pumpkin. He stir-fries whatever vegetables he finds, eating them with rice from a twenty-five-kilogram bag. He is learning this land, adjusting his diet with the seasons, making a crab trap to catch some of summer's bounty of Dungeness.

He takes what he needs, nothing more.

A few months ago, desperate and out of work, he found himself on a fishing vessel off the coast, trapped for weeks with addicts and ex-cons, angry, troubled and volatile men getting through this stretch of tough, dirty work in a tough, dirty life in a daze of heroin.

Once, my brother was a boy trapped on a farm with the unstable and unpredictable man who was our father. "There was just nowhere to run" is how he spoke of it.

It didn't take long on that ship before he became one of those men. By the time he stepped ashore, he had lost the will to live. He went to bed for six weeks. Lost thirty pounds of muscle. And then ended up in hospital. From there, to detox and then rehab.

Now he is sitting on a rock in a garden telling me that he has to live simply in order to be safe. He has to avoid making too much money. He works long hours on a construction site as a day labourer, earning minimum wage. When I saw my father in Calgary all those years ago, he was doing exactly the same thing. Different men, different reasons, same place.

Micah leads me to a tree. "Apricots," he says, full of wonder. They were just raining down. Incredible.

I point out the nasturtiums. "You can eat those," I tell him.

"The flowers?"

"Make yourself a fancy-pants salad."

He laughs. We both do.

acknowledgements

There are friends and acquaintances too many to name who have brightened my world at different moments along the way. Forgive me for not listing here all those acts of generosity and kindness and limiting individual thanks to those directly related to the text.

My thanks to Tita, Miles, Lola, Vibika, Diana, Tim, Clare, Sonia, Naoko, Scott and Dr. B for reading and commenting on various drafts; to my friends and colleagues at University College for giving me the space in which to write for a year; to Ellen Levine for representing me; and to Kristin Cochrane, Brad Martin, Scott Sellers, Lynn Henry, Tim Rostron, Shaun Oakey and everyone at Doubleday Canada for their tremendous support. I reserve the greatest affection and gratitude for my editor and friend, Martha Kanya-Forstner, with whom I've had the privilege of working now for almost a decade and a half, and who always pushes me to delve deeper than I think I am able to go.

Parts of this memoir have appeared in slightly different forms in the following publications: *Ottawa Citizen*, April 1, 2001; *AWOL: Tales for Travel-Inspired Minds*, Jennifer Barclay and Amy Logan, eds. (Vintage Canada, 2003); *Word Carving: The Craft of Literary Journalism*, Moira Farr and Ian Pearson, eds. (Banff Centre Press, 2003); *The First Man in My Life: Daughters Write about Their Fathers*, Sandra Martin, ed. (Penguin Canada, 2007); *Toronto Life*, May 2011; and *Canadian Living*, December 2012.

In the memoir I quote Isak Dinesen from an interview in *The New York Times Book Review*, November 3, 1957. I also quote from *The Boy in the Moon: A Father's Search for His Disabled Son*, Ian Brown (Vintage Canada, 2010); *The White Album: Essays*, Joan Didion (Farrar, Straus and Giroux, 2009); and *The Year of Magical Thinking*, Joan Didion (Vintage, 2007).